KU-739-039

FIRST TIME

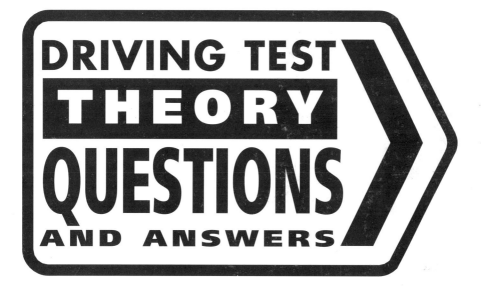

DRIVING TEST
THEORY
QUESTIONS
AND ANSWERS

by

Dr Michael C Cox

AA Publishing

Produced by AA Publishing.

© The Automobile Association 1997
First edition 1996
Reprinted 1996 (5 times)
New edition with revised questions 1997

Crown copyright material reproduced under licence from the
Controller of HMSO and the Driving Standards Agency.

ISBN 0 7495 1689 5

Published by AA Publishing (a trading name of Automobile
Association Developments Limited, whose registered office
is Norfolk House, Priestley Road, Basingstoke, Hampshire
RG24 9NY; registered number 1878835).

The AA's Web site address is www.theaa.co.uk.

The contents of this book are believed correct at the time of
printing. Nevertheless, the publishers cannot be held
responsible for any errors or omissions or for changes in the
details given in this book or for the consequences of any
reliance on the information provided by the same.

Colour separation by Anton Graphics, Andover.
Printed by George Over Limited, London and Rugby.

A RANGE OF PRODUCTS TO HELP YOU
The Associated Examining Board, The National Extension
College and the AA have joined together to produce a range
of teaching and learning products: The Theory Test Open
Learning Pack (NEC) and the Theory Test Classroom Pack
(AEB). You can get information about these products from:

The Associated Examining Board, Development Office,
Stag Hill House, Guildford, Surrey GU2 5XJ

Since July 1996 learner drivers must pass a theory test and a practical test to get a full driving licence.

YOUR QUESTIONS ANSWERED

Q. *Why a theory test?*

A. To check that drivers know and understand what to do before they do it.

Q. *How does it work?*

A. The test consists of 35 multiple-choice questions.

Q. *What is a multiple-choice question?*

A. One with 4, 5 or 6 answers to choose from.

Q. *What does the test cover?*

A. All the topics listed in this book.

ABOUT THIS BOOK

This book will help you to pass your theory test:

- it explains and revises the theory of driving
- it has lots of useful advice and information
- it has all the official questions and answers.

The book is divided into four main sections. The questions are arranged under the 14 official syllabus topics. Questions dealing with related aspects of a topic are grouped together. Notes and explanations follow each question or group of questions. All the correct answers are at the back of the book.

HOW TO USE THIS BOOK

1. Look at the list of topics on page 3 and turn to one you find interesting.
2. Read the first question and tick your choice of answer(s).
3. Study any note or explanation following the question.
4. Check your answer(s) against the correct answers at the back of the book.
5. Make sure you understand the answers before you try the next question.

WARNING

Do **not** try too many questions at once.

Do **not** try to learn the answers by heart.

The order of the answers in this book may be different from how they are arranged in the actual test – so do **not** try to memorise the order.

HOW TO ANSWER THE QUESTIONS

Each question has four, five or six answers. You must mark the boxes with the correct answer or answers. Each question tells you how many answers to mark.

Study each question carefully, making sure you understand. Look carefully at any diagram, drawing or photograph. Before you look at the answers given, decide what you think the right answer may be. You can then select the answer that matches the one you had decided on. If you follow this system, you will avoid being confused by answers which appear to be similar.

You now have to pass two driving tests before you can apply for a full driving licence. The new test, introduced in July 1996, is a written theory test, and this book contains all the **official questions** that you may have to answer. You will have to pass your theory test before you can apply for the practical test.

PREPARING FOR BOTH TESTS

You are strongly recommended to prepare for the theory test at the **same time** as you develop your skills behind the wheel. Obviously, there are many similarities between the two tests – it is all about helping to make you a safer driver on today's busy roads. By preparing for both tests at the same time, you will reinforce your knowledge and understanding of all aspects of driving and you will improve your chances of passing both tests first time.

THE THEORY TEST

You will have 40 minutes to complete the paper and all questions are multiple-choice. The Government may change the pass mark from time to time. Your driving school will be able to tell you if there has been a change. Also, the Government may, from time to time, introduce new or amended questions. However, if you are fully prepared on each topic, you will be in a position to answer any question.

SELECTING A DRIVING SCHOOL

When you select a driving school to teach you the practical skills, make sure they are prepared to advise and help you with the theory test. Good driving schools will provide theory practice papers for you to complete before you take the real test. These papers will help you judge your level of knowledge and help with your preparation. Check with friends who have been taught recently, and make sure you understand the difference between an instructor who displays a pink badge (a trainee instructor) and one who displays a green badge (a fully qualified instructor). Price is important, so find out whether the school offers any discounts for blocks or courses of lessons paid in advance; if you decide to pay in advance, make sure the driving school is reputable. If lesson prices are very low, ask yourself 'why?' And don't forget to ask about the car you'll be learning to drive in. Is it modern and reliable? Is it insured?

WHAT TO EXPECT

As with all courses, there are a number of subjects you will need to master. All good driving schools will have available a progress sheet and syllabus which sets out all the skills you will need and keeps a record of your progress. You will probably find that if you take a two-hour lesson every week, your rate of progress will surprise you!

It is important to book and take your theory test at an early stage in your course of practical lessons.

After a few hours of tuition the instructor will discuss with you a structured course to suit your needs and you can agree on the likely date when you will be ready to take the practical test. You can then apply for a practical test appointment; this will give you added incentive to prepare thoroughly.

THE AA'S DRIVING SCHOOL

The AA has a driving school staffed by fully qualified instructors, who are all familiar with this book, the theory test and the practical test. Why not give them a try? You can ring for details on freephone 0800 60 70 80.

KNOWLEDGE, SKILLS AND ATTITUDE

Being a good driver is more than just having the knowledge and the skills – it is about applying them with the right attitude. No one is a 'natural' or a 'perfect driver'. All drivers make mistakes. Being careful, courteous and considerate to other road users will complement the skills and knowledge you will acquire in the coming weeks and make you a good driver.

Preface by **Linda Hatswell** and **Nick Bravery** – AA The Driving School

The four topics in this section are about **you**. The first two are about your abilities as a driver. The last two are about other road users and your attitude towards them.

ALERTNESS

Good drivers are **alert**. This means you must stay wide awake and on the lookout for danger. You must *concentrate* on your driving. You must *observe* and *be aware* of what is happening all around to *anticipate* the actions of other road users and deal with any danger – hidden or in view. You cannot afford to become bored or distracted. Lost concentration causes loss of life.

HAZARD AWARENESS

Good drivers are **perceptive**. They see and hear danger. Sometimes they may even feel and smell it. To be a perceptive driver you must do more than just look and listen. You must constantly *scan* the road well ahead. You must *process* all the information you see and hear in order to *detect, identify* and *interpret* all the hazards.

Good drivers are skilled at **judging** and **deciding** what to do. They adjust their position and speed to gain time for dealing with any hazard in the best way. For hazards involving other road users, good drivers will judge and decide when to speed up, move forward and take priority and when to slow down, hold back and give priority.

Colour blindness or deafness should not prevent you from passing your test but could make driving more difficult and hazardous. If you need spectacles or contact lenses, you must wear them. It is an offence to drive with uncorrected eyesight. Impairment is anything that reduces or weakens our abilities and senses. Our sight, hearing and other abilities often become impaired as we get older. That is why drivers must renew their licence at age 70 and sign a declaration of their fitness when they renew their licence every three years after that.

Ill-health and medication can impair your driving. Anyone suffering from daytime epilepsy is not allowed even a provisional driving licence. If you are diabetic you should avoid driving if you have not eaten for two hours. Stress and tiredness can impair your driving. Accidents are frequently caused by drivers falling asleep at the wheel.

Alcohol, even in very small amounts, can seriously affect your driving. The legal limits of alcohol are 35 micrograms per 100 ml of breath, 80 milligrams per 100 ml of blood and 107 milligrams per 100 ml of urine. It is an offence to refuse to give a specimen for an alcohol test. You will lose your licence if you are over the limit when driving or just in charge of a motor vehicle. You can be charged with a drink driving offence even if you are below the legal limit. Some drugs can affect your driving ability, and you should check before taking any drugs or medication whether it is safe for you to drive.

VULNERABLE ROAD USERS

People cause 95% of all road accidents. Pedestrians, cyclists, moped riders, motorcyclists and motorists are all road users. Young children and elderly or disabled people with slow reactions are especialy vulnerable. A pedestrian in a dark coat is not very conspicuous at night. The same is true of a cyclist without lights! You must watch out for cyclists, especially younger ones. They may suddenly veer sideways and they are easily blown off course by wind and rain. Moped riders and motorcyclists are less affected by weather but they can be as vulnerable as cyclists. Buses, coaches, large vehicles and articulated lorries present their drivers with different problems. They need time to speed up or slow down, and room to manoeuvre. Remember that passengers stepping from a bus or coach could become pedestrians on the road ahead of you.

ATTITUDE

To be a good driver, you must be **courteous** and **considerate** towards other road users. You must recognise the value of eye contact. You must be aware of the risks to pedestrians and cyclists. You should keep safe distances from other vehicles and give priority where appropriate. You should realise that some road users, like the newly qualified licence holder, will lack experience. Some drivers, like the elderly and the disabled, may be at a disadvantage. They may rely on you for their safety.

Q 1 What, according to The Highway Code, do the letters MSM mean?

Mark one answer

- **A.** Mirror, signal, manoeuvre
- **B.** Manoeuvre, signal, mirror
- **C.** Mirror, speed, manoeuvre
- **D.** Manoeuvre, speed, mirror

A manoeuvre is any change, no matter how small, in your speed and/or direction. A hazard is anything that may cause you to alter your speed and/or direction. Good drivers use their mirrors to monitor the traffic behind them and to help them decide in good time on the need to signal their intentions to other road users. Remember that your brake lights will signal your intention to slow down. The routine for normal driving is MSM–PSL because your manoeuvre gives you a better Position and Speed to Look for hazards.

Q 2 What is meant by 'defensive' driving?

Mark one answer

- **A.** Being alert and thinking ahead
- **B.** Always driving slowly and gently
- **C.** Always letting others go first
- **D.** Pulling over for faster traffic

Defensive drivers are constantly on the alert to assess the traffic situation and the dangers all around them. They use their mirrors before signalling any manoeuvre to give them a better position and/or speed to reassess the hazards and the traffic.

Q 3 You may drive on the footpath

Mark one answer

- **A.** To overtake slow-moving traffic
- **B.** When the pavement is very wide
- **C.** If no pedestrians are near
- **D.** To get into a property

Always be on the alert for pedestrians, especially where driveways cross pavements or footpaths. Take care not to cause an obstruction to pedestrians and other road users by inconsiderate parking on a driveway or by illegal parking on a pavement or footpath. Just think how dangerous this could be to a blind pedestrian.

Q 4 To move off safely from a parked position you should

Mark one answer

- **A.** Signal if other drivers will need to slow down
- **B.** NOT look round if there is a parked vehicle close in front of you
- **C.** Give a hand signal as well as using your indicators
- **D.** Use your mirrors and look round for a final check

Your signal shows what you intend to do. So you must signal correctly at the right time. Before you signal, make sure it is safe to do whatever you intend. For example, only when there is a safe gap in the traffic should you signal your intention to move off. Your signal to other traffic is a warning **not** an order. You **cannot** tell other road users what to do.

Q 5 What is the safest way to brake?

Mark one answer

- [ ] **A.** Brake lightly, then harder as you begin to stop, then ease off just before stopping
- [ ] **B.** Brake hard, put your gear lever into neutral and pull your handbrake on just before stopping
- [ ] **C.** Brake lightly, push your clutch pedal down and pull your handbrake on just before stopping
- [ ] **D.** Put your gear lever into neutral, brake hard, then ease off just before stopping

> Never brake hard except in a real emergency; brake progressively. Keep in gear for as long as possible. When the car has stopped, use the handbrake to set the rear brakes.

Q 6 You are driving on a wet road. You have to stop your vehicle in an emergency. You should

Mark one answer

- [ ] **A.** Apply the handbrake and footbrake together
- [ ] **B.** Keep both hands on the wheel
- [ ] **C.** Select reverse gear
- [ ] **D.** Give an arm signal

> Real emergencies are rare. Most of the time when we brake sharply and stop suddenly we have failed to plan ahead and spot the hazards early enough to brake progressively. Remember that stopping distances on a wet road are at least double those on a dry road.

Q 7 You may remove your seat belt when carrying out a manoeuvre that involves

Mark one answer

- [ ] **A.** Reversing
- [ ] **B.** A hill start
- [ ] **C.** An emergency stop
- [ ] **D.** Driving slowly

> Look where you are going. When going forwards driving normally, this means looking through your front window most of the time. When going backwards driving in reverse, this means looking through your rear window most of the time. Steering with one hand and holding the passenger seat with the other hand can make it easier to look out of the rear window. A hill start, an emergency stop and reversing are exercises included in the practical driving test.

Q 8 When you're NOT sure that it's safe to reverse your vehicle you should

Mark one answer

- [ ] **A.** Use your horn
- [ ] **B.** Rev your engine
- [ ] **C.** Get out and check
- [ ] **D.** Reverse slowly

> It is tragic but true that people have been killed or seriously injured when struck by a vehicle being driven slowly in reverse gear. Young children, elderly and disabled people are especially vulnerable, often because they may not be aware of any danger.

Q 9 You are reversing from a driveway and cannot see clearly. There are many pedestrians around. You should

Mark one answer

- [ ] **A.** Continue whilst sounding your horn
- [ ] **B.** Continue with your hazard lights on
- [ ] **C.** Get someone to guide you
- [ ] **D.** Continue: it is your right of way

It is much safer to reverse from a road into a driveway in order later to be able to drive forward from the driveway into the road. Traffic on a road should normally be given priority over vehicles emerging from a driveway. Except in a motorway emergency, you should not switch on your hazard warning lights when your vehicle is moving.

Q 10 You want to reverse into a side road. You are not sure that the area behind your car is clear. What should you do?

Mark one answer

- [ ] **A.** Look through the rear window only
- [ ] **B.** Get out and check
- [ ] **C.** Check the mirrors only
- [ ] **D.** Carry on, assuming it's clear

Before you can reverse into a side road you must go past it and stop in a convenient position. As you pass the turning, drive slowly and glance into the side road to check that the area is clear. Keep a sharp lookout for vulnerable road users and be ready to give priority to approaching traffic in the side road.

Q 11 You're reversing your vehicle into a side road. When would the greatest hazard to passing traffic occur?

Mark one answer

- [ ] **A.** After you have completed the manoeuvre
- [ ] **B.** Just before you actually begin the manoeuvre
- [ ] **C.** After you have entered the side road
- [ ] **D.** When the front of your vehicle swings out

Just before you start to turn in reverse into the side road you should check for any traffic approaching in the main road. Remember that on a road for two-way traffic, anyone approaching you from the opposite side of the main road cannot see your reversing lights and will not necessarily expect the front of your vehicle to swing towards them as you reverse around the corner.

Q 12 When turning your car in the road, you should

Mark one answer

- [ ] **A.** Overhang the kerb
- [ ] **B.** Use a driveway if possible
- [ ] **C.** Check all around for other road users
- [ ] **D.** Keep your hand on the handbrake throughout

Whatever you are doing, you must be alert and show consideration for other road users. You should choose a safe and convenient place if you need to turn in the road. Do not put pedestrians in danger. Do not inconvenience other road users.

Q 13 You may make a U-turn

Mark one answer

- **A.** When it is safe on a wide road
- **B.** On a motorway, when it is safe
- **C.** In a wide one-way street
- **D.** By mounting both pavements carefully

Motorways are for one-way traffic only. It is extremely dangerous and a serious offence to drive the wrong way down a one-way street or on a motorway. Remember that pavements are for pedestrians. It is never safe to make a U-turn at a junction no matter how wide the roads are at the junction.

Q 14 While driving, you intend to turn left into a minor road. On the approach you should

Mark one answer

- **A.** Keep just left of the middle of the road
- **B.** Keep in the middle of the road
- **C.** Swing out wide just before turning
- **D.** Keep well to the left of the road

The road position in normal driving is on the left, keeping to the left and staying well clear of traffic coming from the opposite direction. Only long, large vehicles need to swing out wide, and then only just before turning.

Q 15 You are driving on a main road. You intend to turn right into a side road. Just before turning you should

Mark one answer

- **A.** Adjust your interior mirror
- **B.** Flash your headlamps
- **C.** Steer over to the left
- **D.** Check for traffic overtaking on your offside

Always check and, if necessary, adjust all your mirrors as part of your daily routine at the start of the day. If they ever need readjusting during the day, pull over and park in a safe, convenient place before attempting to readjust them. Only long, large vehicles need to swing left when they are turning right into a side road.

Q 16 You want to turn right from a main road into a side road. Just before turning you should

Mark one answer

- **A.** Cancel your right-turn signal
- **B.** Select first gear
- **C.** Check for traffic overtaking on your right
- **D.** Stop and set the handbrake

If traffic is approaching from the opposite direction, you may need to wait with the right-hand indicators on, the handbrake set, the clutch down and your vehicle in first gear. But when your way forward is clear it is vital to check for traffic from behind before you start to turn.

Q 17 Motorcyclists will often look round over their right shoulder just before turning right. This is because

Mark one answer

- [ ] **A.** They need to listen for following traffic
- [ ] **B.** Motorcycles do not have mirrors
- [ ] **C.** Looking around helps them balance as they turn
- [ ] **D.** They need to check for traffic in their blind area

Mirrors cannot show motorists and motorcyclists everything that is happening behind them. When you see a cyclist or motorcyclist up ahead you should always be prepared for the rider to change speed and/or direction. Riders do not always glance back or even signal before turning.

Q 18 Which of the following are hazards motorcyclists present in queues of traffic?

Mark three answers

- [ ] **A.** Cutting in just in front of you
- [ ] **B.** Riding in single file
- [ ] **C.** Passing very close to your car
- [ ] **D.** Riding with their headlamp on dipped beam
- [ ] **E.** Filtering between the lanes

Motorcycles are not as manoeuvrable as bicycles but they can move much faster and their riders are just as vulnerable as cyclists. In slow-moving traffic you should watch for the possibility of riders overtaking your vehicle on the nearside.

Q 19 You are driving in slow-moving queues of traffic. Just before changing lane you should

Mark one answer

- [ ] **A.** Sound the horn
- [ ] **B.** Look for motorcyclists filtering through the traffic
- [ ] **C.** Give a 'slowing down' arm signal
- [ ] **D.** Change down to first gear

When you are in a traffic queue, be patient and think carefully before changing lanes. If you really need to change lanes, make sure you use your mirrors and give an appropriate signal in good time.

Q 20 In which of these situations should you avoid overtaking?

Mark one answer

- [ ] **A.** Just after a bend
- [ ] **B.** In a one-way street
- [ ] **C.** On a 30mph road
- [ ] **D.** Approaching a dip in the road

Overtaking is potentially the most dangerous manoeuvre because it often puts you in the path of traffic coming from the opposite direction at a high relative speed. For example, two cars travelling at 60mph will approach one another at a relative speed of 120mph so that the gap between them is closing at about 12 car lengths every second. If you must overtake, remember that the normal MSM–PSL routine becomes the PSL–MSM routine for overtaking. You need the best Position and Speed to Look ahead and in your Mirror before you Signal your intention to begin the overtaking Manoeuvre.

Q 21 You are driving at night and are dazzled by the headlights of an oncoming car. You should

Mark one answer

- **A.** Slow down or stop
- **B.** Close your eyes
- **C.** Flash your headlights
- **D.** Pull down the sun visor

Keep your eyes open and on the road. Try to avoid looking directly at oncoming headlights. Do not dazzle other road users: dip your headlights in good time.

Q 22 You are driving a vehicle fitted with a hand-held telephone. To answer the telephone you MUST

Mark one answer

- **A.** Find a safe place to stop
- **B.** Reduce your speed
- **C.** Steer the car with one hand
- **D.** Be particularly careful at junctions

Q 23 You should only use a hand-held telephone when

Mark one answer

- **A.** Your vehicle has an automatic gear change
- **B.** Driving at low speeds
- **C.** You have stopped at a safe place
- **D.** Travelling on minor roads

You must stop to use a hand-held telephone. You may only stop on the hard shoulder of a motorway in a **real** emergency. You cannot pay proper attention to your driving if you are using any telephone. See **Q50**.

Q 24 When approaching a hazard your FIRST reaction should be to

Mark one answer

- **A.** Use your footbrake
- **B.** Change direction
- **C.** Release the accelerator
- **D.** Check the mirrors

A hazard is anything that could cause you to alter your speed and/or direction. Good drivers are alert to the dangers behind them as well as the hazards ahead of them.

Q 25 A rumble device is designed to

Mark two answers

- **A.** Give directions
- **B.** Prevent cattle escaping
- **C.** Alert drivers to low tyre pressure
- **D.** Alert drivers to a hazard
- **E.** Encourage drivers to reduce speed

Raised markings, strips or studs on the roadway cause a judder you can feel in your steering wheel and a rumbling noise you can hear inside your vehicle. Rumble devices are used on motorways to warn you of serious hazards. You ignore these warnings at your peril. See **Q461** and **Q463**.

Q 26 What THREE things should the driver of the grey car be specially aware of?

Always look ahead. Watch out for pedestrians, especially young children, elderly and disabled people. They can appear from nowhere and step into your path without warning. You must also watch for other moving hazards such as car doors suddenly opening and vehicles moving off without any indication. You must also keep an eye on vehicles following behind you and make sure you do not put them in any danger by acting unpredictably. See **Q393**.

Mark three answers

- **A.** Pedestrians stepping out between cars
- **B.** The bumpy road surface
- **C.** Empty parking spaces
- **D.** Other cars behind the grey car
- **E.** Cars leaving parking spaces
- **F.** Parked cars' doors opening

Q 27 What are TWO main hazards a driver should be aware of when driving along this street?

Mark two answers

- **A.** Glare from the sun
- **B.** Car doors opening suddenly
- **C.** Lack of road markings
- **D.** The headlights on parked cars being switched on
- **E.** Large goods vehicles
- **F.** Children running out from between vehicles

Q 28 What should the driver of the red car do?

Mark one answer

- **A.** Wave on the pedestrians who are waiting to cross
- **B.** Wait for the pedestrian in the road to cross
- **C.** Quickly drive behind the pedestrian in the road
- **D.** Tell the pedestrian in the road she should not have crossed

You must always give priority to pedestrians in danger on the road. Remember how vulnerable they are. If you are stopping for pedestrians to cross, signal your intentions properly to other road users. Make eye contact with the pedestrians but do not wave them across. You have no authority to tell others what to do. You can only tell others what **you** intend to do.

Q 29 What should the driver of the car approaching the crossing do?

Mark one answer

- [ ] **A.** Continue at the same speed
- [ ] **B.** Sound the horn
- [ ] **C.** Drive through quickly
- [ ] **D.** Slow down and get ready to stop

Approach crossings with care especially when pedestrians are waiting or seem about to step into the road. Be prepared to slow down. Remember to use your mirror and signal your intentions to other road users. Make eye contact with the pedestrians and give a proper arm signal. Do not wave them on to the crossing. See **Q551**.

Q 30 Where would you expect to see these markers?

Mark two answers

- [ ] **A.** On a motorway sign
- [ ] **B.** At the entrance to a narrow bridge
- [ ] **C.** On a large goods vehicle
- [ ] **D.** On a builder's skip placed on the road

These markers show up at night or on an overcast day by reflecting back the light from your headlamps. Always take care when you approach and overtake them.

Q 31 Which road user has caused a hazard?

Mark one answer

- [ ] **A.** The parked car (arrowed A)
- [ ] **B.** The pedestrian waiting to cross (arrowed B)
- [ ] **C.** The moving car (arrowed C)
- [ ] **D.** The car turning (arrowed D)

It is normally an offence to stop within the area marked by zigzag lines because it increases the dangers to pedestrians using the crossing by obstructing the view of other road users. You must not stop in that area even to pick up or set down a disabled passenger. See **Q599**, **Q136**, **Q137** and **Q380**.

Q 32 What is the main hazard shown in this picture?

Mark one answer

- [ ] **A.** Vehicles turning right
- [ ] **B.** Vehicles doing U-turns
- [ ] **C.** The cyclist crossing the road
- [ ] **D.** Parked cars around the corner

Always watch for the road user doing the unexpected. On dual carriageways right turns may be allowed but not U-turns and parking. Cyclists may be allowed to use the dual carriageway but not to cross the lanes in the path of oncoming traffic as seems likely here. Crossing at the traffic lights would be much safer.

Q 33 What is the main hazard a driver should be aware of when following this cyclist?

Mark one answer

- [ ] **A.** The cyclist may move into the left gap and dismount
- [ ] **B.** The cyclist may swerve out into the road
- [ ] **C.** The contents of the cyclist's carrier may fall on to the road
- [ ] **D.** The cyclist may wish to turn right at the end of the road

Always be prepared for a cyclist to change direction without warning. Be patient and hold back until you can overtake safely. Keep enough distance between you and the cyclist so that you could stop your vehicle in good time.

Q 34 Following a large goods vehicle too closely is dangerous because

Mark one answer

- [ ] **A.** Your field of vision is seriously reduced
- [ ] **B.** Slipstreaming will reduce wind effect
- [ ] **C.** Your engine will overheat
- [ ] **D.** Your brakes need a constant cooling effect

If you keep a safe distance from a large vehicle you are following, you will be in a better position to assess if it is safe to overtake and the driver is more likely to see your signal when you decide to overtake. Remember the special routine PSL–MSM.

Q 35 You see this sign on the rear of a slow-moving lorry that you want to pass. It is travelling in the middle of the road. You should

Mark one answer
- [ ] **A.** Cautiously approach the lorry then pass on either side
- [ ] **B.** Follow the lorry until you can leave the motorway
- [ ] **C.** Wait on the hard shoulder until the lorry has stopped
- [ ] **D.** Approach with care and keep to the left of the lorry

---

Vehicles engaged in road or motorway maintenance may display a sign indicating on which side traffic should overtake. Be prepared to avoid putting at risk any workmen operating near by.

Q 36 The driver of which car has caused a hazard?

Mark one answer
- [ ] **A.** Car A
- [ ] **B.** Car B
- [ ] **C.** Car C
- [ ] **D.** Car D

At a STOP sign you **must stop** – not behind or over, but **at** the solid **white line**. Car A has forced other cars to move on to the diagonal white hazard markings for the right-turn lane.

Q 37 What is the main hazard the driver of the red car (arrowed) should be most aware of?

Mark one answer
- [ ] **A.** Glare from the sun may affect the driver's vision
- [ ] **B.** The black car may stop suddenly
- [ ] **C.** The bus may move out into the road
- [ ] **D.** Oncoming vehicles will assume the driver is turning right

---

Always look ahead for the possibility of buses and coaches pulling in or moving off. Remember that these large vehicles are often difficult to manoeuvre and their drivers have poorer vision behind them. The red car could well be in the bus driver's blind spot.

Q 38 What should the driver of the red car (arrowed) do?

Mark one answer
- **A.** Sound the horn to tell other drivers where he is
- **B.** Squeeze through the gap
- **C.** Wave the driver of the white car to go on
- **D.** Wait until the car blocking the way has moved

Drivers should be patient. The driver of the red car should, if possible, make eye contact with the other car drivers. It is then up to those drivers to decide when it is safe for them to move. The driver should sound the horn only if other moving vehicles pose a danger. See **Q269**, **Q270** and **Q595**.

Q 39 What should the driver of the grey car (arrowed) do?

Mark one answer
- **A.** Cross if the way is clear
- **B.** Reverse out of the box junction
- **C.** Wait in the same place until the lights are green
- **D.** Wait until the lights are red then cross

You may enter a yellow box junction if you want to turn right and are only prevented by oncoming vehicles or by others turning right. Otherwise, you must not enter until your exit road or lane from the box junction is clear. The same basic rule applies to all junctions: do not proceed unless your way forward is clear. See **Q406** and **Q407**.

Q 40 As you approach this bridge you should

Mark three answers
- **A.** Move into the middle of the road to get a better view
- **B.** Slow down
- **C.** Get over the bridge as quickly as possible
- **D.** Consider using your horn
- **E.** Find another route
- **F.** Beware of pedestrians

The greatest hazards are the ones you cannot see. Remember the PSL routine: the best Position to see the danger and the Speed to let you stop and allow time to Look before you reach the danger. See **Q20** and **Q544**.

Q 41 What should the driver of a car coming up to this level crossing do?

Mark one answer

- **A.** Drive through quickly
- **B.** Drive through carefully
- **C.** Stop before the barrier
- **D.** Switch on hazard warning lights

A steady amber light always means **stop**. At railway crossings the steady amber light is usually followed immediately by two flashing red lights. You should keep going if you have already crossed the white line when the amber light comes on. But you **must not** cross the line when the red lights are flashing even if a train has gone by. It is only safe to cross when the lights go off and the barriers open.

Q 42 In heavy motorway traffic you're being followed closely by the vehicle behind. How can you lower the risk of an accident?

Mark one answer

- **A.** Increase your distance from the vehicle in front
- **B.** Tap your foot on the brake pedal
- **C.** Switch on your hazard lights
- **D.** Move on to the hard shoulder and stop

You control the gap between you and the vehicle in front of yours. You cannot control the distance between you and the vehicle behind you. Always try to let dangerous drivers get in front of you where you can see them. Remember you are not in a race. Anyway, racing on the public highway is a serious offence in the eyes of the law.

Q 43 To drive legally you must be able to read a number plate from what distance?

Mark one answer
- **A.** 10 metres (33 feet)
- **B.** 15 metres (50 feet)
- **C.** 20.5 metres (67 feet)
- **D.** 205 metres (673 feet)

You should be able to read the number plate on a vehicle about four or five cars away from you. And you should regard this as a minimum requirement. It is sensible to have your eyes tested regularly, especially as you get older.

Q 44 A driver can only read a number plate at the required distance with glasses on. The glasses should be worn

Mark one answer
- **A.** All the time when driving
- **B.** Only when driving long distances
- **C.** Only when reversing
- **D.** Only in poor visibility

Q 45 You find that you need glasses to read vehicle number plates. When must you wear them?

Mark one answer
- **A.** Only in bad weather conditions
- **B.** At all times when driving
- **C.** Only when you think it necessary
- **D.** Only in bad light or at night time

You must wear your glasses (or contact lenses) at all times when you are driving if you need them to pass the official eyesight test. If you drive without them you put yourself and others at risk.

Q 46 When driving towards a bright setting sun, glare can be reduced by

Mark one answer
- **A.** Closing one eye
- **B.** Dipping the interior mirror
- **C.** Wearing dark glasses
- **D.** Looking sideways

Most vehicles are fitted with visors to reduce the effect of glare. Whenever you use a solid visor, always pivot it fully down and forward to avoid hitting your head on its edge. Remember that it may be dangerous to wear sun glasses on a dark, cloudy day or at night.

Q 47 You're about to drive home. You can't find the glasses you need to wear when driving. You should

Mark one answer
- **A.** Drive home slowly, keeping to quiet roads
- **B.** Borrow a friend's glasses and drive home
- **C.** Drive home at night, so that the lights will help you
- **D.** Find a way of getting home without driving

If you wear the wrong glasses you could still put people in danger and be guilty of an offence. With uncorrected eyesight, driving at night is even more difficult than driving in daylight.

Q 48 You are planning to drive a long distance. Which THREE things will make the journey safer?

Mark three answers
- **A.** Avoid travelling at night
- **B.** Ensure a supply of fresh air
- **C.** Avoid motorways
- **D.** Make stops for refreshments
- **E.** Drive slowly

At night your view ahead may be limited by the beam of your headlights. And there is always the danger of dazzle by the headlights of oncoming vehicles. Driving slowly does not necessarily mean driving safely. In general you should try to fit in with the traffic flow according to the conditions and speed limits in force. Motorways can be very safe but you must guard against becoming bored or tired.

Q 49 Which TWO things would help to keep you alert during a long journey?

Mark two answers
- **A.** Finish your journey as fast as you can
- **B.** Keep off the motorways and use country roads
- **C.** Make sure that you get plenty of fresh air
- **D.** Make regular stops for refreshments

Driving for too long and without fresh air is dangerous. Falling asleep at the wheel causes injury and death on all kinds of roads. Be safe. Break your long journey into stages and avoid heavy meals which will make you sleepy. Strong coffee could help to keep you awake but fresh air and a short rest may be all you need. Avoid too much liquid refreshment and always avoid alcoholic drinks.

Q 50 Which THREE are likely to make you lose concentration while driving?

Mark three answers
- **A.** Looking at road maps
- **B.** Listening to loud music
- **C.** Using your windscreen washers
- **D.** Looking in your wing mirror
- **E.** Using a mobile phone

Keep your hands on the steering wheel, your eyes on the road and your ears open when driving. A moment's loss of concentration can be the difference between life and death for you and other road users. Keep your windscreen clean. Keep your mirrors properly adjusted and use them to check on the actions of following traffic.

Q 51 A driver pulls out of a side road in front of you. You have to brake hard. You should

Mark one answer
- **A.** Ignore the error and stay calm
- **B.** Flash your lights to show your annoyance
- **C.** Sound your horn to show your annoyance
- **D.** Overtake as soon as possible

Whenever we have to brake suddenly or hard we should ask ourselves 'why?' The honest answer is usually that we were driving too fast for the conditions and failing to anticipate the hazards ahead. Good drivers are quick to blame themselves for their errors of judgement and slow to blame others for their mistakes.

Q 52 A car driver pulls out causing you to brake. You should

Mark one answer

- **A.** Keep calm and not retaliate
- **B.** Overtake and sound your horn
- **C.** Drive close behind and sound your horn
- **D.** Flag the driver down and explain the mistake

When another road user makes a mistake and causes us a problem we easily forget those occasions when we made a mistake and caused someone else a problem. All we can ever hope to do is set other road users the best example of our own good driving.

Q 53 Another driver does something that upsets you. You should

Mark one answer

- **A.** Try not to react
- **B.** Let them know how you feel
- **C.** Flash your headlamps several times
- **D.** Sound your horn

Q 54 Another driver's behaviour has upset you. It may help if you

Mark one answer

- **A.** Stop and take a break
- **B.** Shout abusive language
- **C.** Gesture to them with your hand
- **D.** Follow their car, flashing the headlights

Good drivers stay calm. They do not react angrily to the actions of bad drivers. To be a good defensive driver you must be in control of your thoughts and actions. You must also stay alert and be prepared to avoid the dangerous actions of inconsiderate road users. Remember that you cannot control what other people do. All you can do is set a good example.

Q 55 How often should you stop on a long journey?

Mark one answer

- **A.** When you need petrol
- **B.** At least every four hours
- **C.** At least every two hours
- **D.** When you need to eat

For some people, including new and inexperienced drivers, even a one-hour journey can be too long without a break. Instructors usually divide a lesson into sections so that pupils are not driving for an extended period without a break.

Q 56 If you are feeling tired it is best to stop as soon as you can. Until then you should

Mark one answer

- **A.** Increase your speed to find a stopping place quickly
- **B.** Ensure a supply of fresh air
- **C.** Gently tap the steering wheel
- **D.** Keep changing speed to improve concentration

There is no substitute for fresh air. Do not let the inside of your vehicle become hot and stuffy. The lack of oxygen will make you drowsy and fall asleep without warning.

Q 57 You are driving on a motorway. You feel tired. You should

Mark one answer

- **A.** Carry on but drive slowly
- **B.** Leave the motorway at the next exit
- **C.** Complete your journey as quickly as possible
- **D.** Stop on the hard shoulder

You may **only** stop on the hard shoulder **if there is an emergency**. This means some danger arises after you join the motorway. Feeling tired is **not** an emergency in the eyes of the law because you could leave the motorway when you begin to feel drowsy.

Q 58 Your reactions will be much slower when driving

Mark one answer

- **A.** If tired
- **B.** In fog
- **C.** Too quickly
- **D.** In rain

Q 59 You have taken medication that may make you feel drowsy. Your friends tell you it is safe to drive. What should you do?

Mark one answer

- **A.** Take their advice and drive
- **B.** Ignore your friends' advice and do not drive
- **C.** Only drive if they come with you
- **D.** Drive for short distances only

Never put yourself and others at risk by driving if you are tired or actually suffering from anything that affects your performance. People prone to hay fever may drive if they are not suffering from an attack or if their medication does not affect their driving. Remember that medicine takes time to act and accidents happen even on short journeys.

Q 60 Your doctor has given you a course of medicine. Why should you ask if it is OK to drive?

Mark one answer

- **A.** Drugs make you a better driver by quickening your reactions
- **B.** You'll have to let your insurance company know about the medicine
- **C.** Some types of medicine can cause your reactions to slow down
- **D.** The medicine you take may affect your eyesight

You must inform your insurance company and the DVLA of any medical condition likely to prevent you from holding a driving licence. If you have any doubt about your fitness you should consult your doctor. Remember that some medicines, including aspirin and paracetamol, may adversely affect your driving performance.

Q 61 You are not sure if your cough medicine will affect your driving. What TWO things could you do?

Mark two answers

- **A.** Ask your doctor
- **B.** Check the medicine label
- **C.** Drive if you feel all right
- **D.** Ask a friend or relative for advice

Q 62 You are taking drugs that are likely to affect your driving. What should you do?

Mark one answer

- **A.** Seek medical advice before driving
- **B.** Limit your driving to essential journeys
- **C.** Only drive if accompanied by a full licence-holder
- **D.** Drive only for short distances

Q 63 You take some cough medicine given to you by a friend. What must you do before driving?

Mark one answer

- **A.** Drink some strong coffee
- **B.** Ask your friend if taking the medicine affected their driving
- **C.** Check the label to see if the medicine will affect your driving
- **D.** Make a short journey to see if the medicine's affecting your driving

> If you take medicine that might affect your driving, consult your doctor before you drive. The next best thing to do is check the label for any advice or warnings. If in doubt, do not drive.

Q 64 How does alcohol affect your driving?

Mark one answer

- **A.** It speeds up your reactions
- **B.** It increases your awareness
- **C.** It improves your co-ordination
- **D.** It reduces your concentration

Q 65 What are THREE ways that drinking alcohol can affect driving?

Mark three answers

- **A.** It slows down your reactions
- **B.** It reduces your co-ordination
- **C.** It affects your judgement of speed
- **D.** It reduces your confidence

Q 66 Which THREE result from drinking alcohol and driving?

Mark three answers

- **A.** Less control
- **B.** A false sense of confidence
- **C.** Faster reactions
- **D.** Poor judgement of speed
- **E.** Greater awareness of danger

Q 67 Which THREE of these are likely effects of drinking alcohol on driving?

Mark three answers

- **A.** Reduced co-ordination
- **B.** Increased confidence
- **C.** Poor judgement
- **D.** Increased concentration
- **E.** Faster reactions
- **F.** Colour blindness

> EFFECTS OF ALCOHOL ON DRIVERS
>
> Alcohol is a depressant. It will reduce your muscle control, blur your vision, lower your concentration and decrease your awareness, especially after dark. Alcohol can give you a false confidence which makes you overestimate your driving ability and performance. You misjudge speeds and distances, and you think your reactions are faster than they really are. Even a small amount of alcohol can impair your driving.

Q 68 Which one of the following is NOT affected by alcohol?

Mark one answer

- [ ] **A.** Judgement of speed
- [ ] **B.** Reaction time
- [ ] **C.** Perception of colours
- [ ] **D.** Co-ordination

Q 69 A driver attends a social event. What precaution should the driver take?

Mark one answer

- [ ] **A.** Drink plenty of coffee after drinking alcohol
- [ ] **B.** Avoid busy roads after drinking alcohol
- [ ] **C.** Avoid drinking alcohol completely
- [ ] **D.** Avoid drinking alcohol on an empty stomach

ALCOHOL AND FOOD

Fatty food in the stomach slows the absorption of alcohol. The more slowly the alcohol is absorbed into the blood stream, the lower is the maximum level attained. Therefore, eating fatty food can lower the maximum level that alcohol could reach in your blood. Never drink quickly on an empty stomach. But remember that even a small amount of alcohol in your blood will affect your driving. And the effects of alcohol could last for up to 12 hours after you stop drinking. NEVER DRINK AND DRIVE.

Q 70 What advice should you give to a driver who has had a few alcoholic drinks at a party?

Mark one answer

- [ ] **A.** Have a strong cup of coffee and then drive home
- [ ] **B.** Drive home carefully and slowly
- [ ] **C.** Wait a short while and then drive home
- [ ] **D.** Go home by public transport

ALCOHOL FOR MEN AND WOMEN

One man is tall and fat. The other is short and thin. Both men drink a pint of beer. What happens to the alcohol level in their blood? It goes higher in the small man's blood. The same would be true if both drinkers had been women. For a man and woman of the same size and weight, the woman's blood alcohol level would get higher than the man's. Remember you could still be charged with a drink driving offence even if the alcohol in your blood, breath or urine is below the legal limit.

Q 71 When driving, what is the maximum legal level for alcohol in your blood?

Mark one answer

- [ ] **A.** 50mg per 100ml
- [ ] **B.** 60mg per 100ml
- [ ] **C.** 80mg per 100ml
- [ ] **D.** 90mg per 100ml

ALCOHOL AND THE LAW

107 milligrams of alcohol in 100ml of urine, or 35 micrograms of alcohol in 100ml of breath, is equivalent to the legal limit of alcohol in the blood. The penalty for driving, attempting to drive or being in charge of a vehicle while over the legal alcohol limit is automatic disqualification with, possibly, imprisonment for up to 6 months and a fine of up to £5000. It would also be a serious offence to fail to provide a specimen for a police laboratory test. NEVER DRINK AND DRIVE.

Q 72 The maximum prison sentence for the offence of driving while unfit through drink and drugs is

Mark one answer

- **A.** 12 months
- **B.** 18 months
- **C.** 6 months
- **D.** 24 months

Q 73 The offence of causing death whilst driving under the influence of drink or drugs carries the maximum penalty of

Mark one answer

- **A.** Eight years' imprisonment
- **B.** Ten years' imprisonment
- **C.** Twelve years' imprisonment
- **D.** Six years' imprisonment

Motoring offences are criminal offences carrying punishments which range in severity from small fines to heavy fines up to £5000, penalty points leading to disqualification, driving bans up to at least two years and prison sentences of varying length. In addition to the legal consequences of breaking the law, the offender will also suffer personal, social and other financial consequences. See **Q360**.

Q 74 What does this sign warn you to look for?

Mark one answer

- **A.** A school crossing patrol
- **B.** A pedestrian crossing
- **C.** A park
- **D.** School children

The word **School** is usually on a plate underneath the sign to warn that you are approaching a school. If the word **Patrol** is on the plate underneath the sign, you know you are approaching a school crossing patrol. Often there is also a pair of amber lights that are flashing when the crossing patrol is actually there to control the traffic. See **Q550**.

Q 75 How will a school crossing patrol signal you to stop?

Mark one answer

- **A.** By pointing to children on the opposite pavement
- **B.** By displaying a red light
- **C.** By displaying a stop sign
- **D.** By giving you an arm signal

The person in charge of the crossing is authorised to control the traffic by holding up the official STOP – CHILDREN sign. No other signal is approved.

Q 76 You are approaching a school crossing patrol. When this sign is held up you must

Mark one answer

- **A.** Stop and allow any children to cross
- **B.** Stop and beckon the children to cross
- **C.** Stop only if the children are on a pedestrian crossing
- **D.** Stop only when the children are actually crossing the road

Q 77 You see someone step into the road holding this sign. What must you do?

Mark one answer

- **A.** Slow down and look out for children
- **B.** Signal the person to cross
- **C.** Drive carefully round the person
- **D.** Pull up before the person

Always approach with care any school and area such as a recreation park where there may be children. Remember that you **must stop** when you see the STOP – CHILDREN sign.

Q 78 A school crossing patrol shows this sign. What must you do?

Mark one answer

- **A.** Continue if it is safe to do so
- **B.** Slow down and be ready to stop
- **C.** Stop ONLY if children are crossing
- **D.** Stop at all times

The STOP – CHILDREN sign means you **must stop** even if you cannot see any children.

Q 79 Where would you see this sign?

Mark one answer

- **A.** In the window of a car taking children to school
- **B.** At the side of the road
- **C.** At playground areas
- **D.** On the rear of a school bus or coach

Q 80 Where would you see this sign?

Mark one answer

- [ ] **A.** On the approach to a school crossing
- [ ] **B.** At a playground entrance
- [ ] **C.** On a school bus
- [ ] **D.** At a 'pedestrians only' area

> When you approach a bus you should look for this sign and take extra care. Children, especially in a group, can be unaware of the dangers around them. Children are very vulnerable and unpredictable road users.

Q 81 Look at this picture. What is the danger you should be most aware of?

Mark one answer

- [ ] **A.** The ice cream van may move off
- [ ] **B.** The driver of the ice cream van may get out
- [ ] **C.** The car on the left may move off
- [ ] **D.** The child may run out into the road

> Whenever you see an ice cream van, slow down and be prepared for children to appear from nowhere and run into the road ahead of you. Remember children are very vulnerable and often unaware of traffic hazards.

Q 82 You are driving past a line of parked cars. You notice a ball bouncing out into the road ahead. What should you do?

Mark one answer

- [ ] **A.** Continue driving at the same speed and sound your horn
- [ ] **B.** Continue driving at the same speed and flash your headlights
- [ ] **C.** Slow down and be prepared to stop for children
- [ ] **D.** Stop and wave the children across to fetch their ball

> Always scan the road ahead. Look for clues to warn you of unseen hazards. Slow down especially when young children at play might run into the road. Remember they may be unaware of any danger or of your approach. Sounding your horn or flashing your lights would not help. Waving them into the road would make matters worse. See **Q269**, **Q270** and **Q595**.

Q 83 While driving you approach a large puddle that's close to the left-hand kerb. Pedestrians are close to the water. You should

Mark two answers

- **A.** Ignore the puddle
- **B.** Brake suddenly and sound your horn
- **C.** Slow down before the puddle
- **D.** Try to avoid splashing the pedestrians
- **E.** Wave at the pedestrians to keep back

Try to imagine yourself being a pedestrian splashed or soaked by an inconsiderate passing motorist. In normal driving you should always keep a safe distance from the kerb. If traffic conditions force you to drive closer to the kerb, then the closer you are the more slowly you must drive.

Q 84 You are driving past parked cars. You notice a wheel of a bicycle sticking out between them. What should you do?

Mark one answer

- **A.** Accelerate past quickly and sound your horn
- **B.** Slow down and wave the cyclist across
- **C.** Brake sharply and flash your headlights
- **D.** Slow down and be prepared to stop for a cyclist

Pedestrians and cyclists should not expect always to be given priority. However, you must never put vulnerable road users in danger by failing to give them priority. Drive carefully with courtesy and consideration for others.

Q 85 A pedestrian steps out into the road just ahead of you. What should you do FIRST?

Mark one answer

- **A.** Sound your horn
- **B.** Check your mirror
- **C.** Flash your headlights
- **D.** Press the brake

Q 86 You are turning left into a side road. Pedestrians are crossing the road near the junction. You must

Mark one answer

- **A.** Wave them on
- **B.** Sound your horn
- **C.** Switch on your hazard lights
- **D.** Wait for them to cross

You must always give priority to pedestrians in danger on the road ahead. Be patient especially if they are elderly, infirm and unaware of your presence.

Q 87 You are turning left from a main road into a side road. People are already crossing the road into which you're turning. You should

Mark one answer

- **A.** Continue, as it is your right of way
- **B.** Signal to them to continue crossing
- **C.** Wait and allow them to cross
- **D.** Sound your horn to warn them of your presence

Try to make eye contact with other road users but never try to give them instructions. Be patient. Do **not** rev your engine. Do not sound your horn unless there is danger. See **Q269**, **Q270** and **Q595**.

Q 88 You are turning left at a junction. Pedestrians have started to cross the road. You should

Mark one answer

- **A.** Go on, giving them plenty of room
- **B.** Stop and wave at them to cross
- **C.** Blow your horn and proceed
- **D.** Give way to them

Q 89 You are at a road junction, turning into a minor road. There are pedestrians crossing the minor road. You should

Mark one answer

- **A.** Stop and wave the pedestrians across
- **B.** Sound your horn to let the pedestrians know that you are there
- **C.** Give way to the pedestrians who are already crossing
- **D.** Carry on; the pedestrians should give way to you

Always look out for pedestrians crossing a road you want to turn into. A pedestrian about to step into a road may wait if you signal clearly in good time and you make eye contact with the pedestrian. Remember that you are not authorised to tell other road users what to do. So never wave pedestrians to step into the road. They might obey your signal without checking and step under a bus.

Q 90 You are about to reverse into a side road. A pedestrian wishes to cross behind you. You should

Mark one answer

- **A.** Wave to the pedestrian to stop
- **B.** Give way to the pedestrian
- **C.** Wave to the pedestrian to cross
- **D.** Reverse before the pedestrian starts to cross

Give way to pedestrians. This rule applies whether you are driving forward or in reverse. When you are reversing, look out especially for children and elderly people. You may not see small children through your rear window. Elderly people may be slow to move out of the way.

Q 91 You are parking your vehicle in the street. The car parked in front of you is displaying an orange badge. You should

Mark one answer

- **A.** Park close to it to save road space
- **B.** Allow room for a wheelchair
- **C.** Wait until the orange-badge holder returns
- **D.** Park with two wheels on the pavement

Disabled parking permits issued by local authorities for use by disabled drivers or passengers must, like the tax disc, be displayed in the windscreen. The official permit may be accompanied by an orange disabled badge or sticker displayed in the rear windscreen.

Q 92 What action would you take when elderly people are crossing the road?

Elderly people

Mark one answer

- **A.** Wave them across so they know that you've seen them
- **B.** Be patient and allow them to cross in their own time
- **C.** Rev the engine to let them know that you're waiting
- **D.** Tap the horn in case they are hard of hearing

Elderly people may be upset by sudden or loud noises and are unable to walk very quickly. Try to make eye contact and, if appropriate, give an arm signal to indicate what you intend to do. Remember that you are not authorised to tell others what to do.

Q 93 You see a pedestrian carrying a white stick. This shows that the person is

Mark one answer

- **A.** Disabled
- **B.** Deaf
- **C.** Elderly
- **D.** Blind

Q 94 You see a pedestrian with a white stick and two red reflective bands. This means that the person is

Mark one answer

- [ ] **A.** Physically disabled
- [ ] **B.** Deaf and dumb
- [ ] **C.** Blind and dumb
- [ ] **D.** Deaf and blind

Take extra care with people who are blind and deaf. Usually you can tell when pedestrians are blind, or blind and deaf, but not when they are just deaf. Bear that in mind if a pedestrian suddenly steps into the road without looking in your direction.

Q 95 At night you see a pedestrian wearing reflective clothing and carrying a bright red light. What does this mean?

Mark one answer

- [ ] **A.** You are approaching roadworks
- [ ] **B.** You are approaching an organised march
- [ ] **C.** You are approaching a slow-moving vehicle
- [ ] **D.** You are approaching an accident black spot

Pedestrians in the road are extremely vulnerable. Always approach them slowly and cautiously. What would you do if the pedestrian was waving a torch to warn of a traffic accident?

Q 96 You are driving in town. There's a bus at the bus stop on the other side of the road. Why should you be careful?

Mark one answer

- [ ] **A.** The bus may have broken down
- [ ] **B.** Pedestrians may come from behind the bus
- [ ] **C.** The bus may move off suddenly
- [ ] **D.** The bus may remain stationary

When in towns, especially near shops, watch out for pedestrians suddenly appearing from behind parked cars and buses. Drive carefully and be prepared to slow down.

Q 97 Which sign means that there may be people walking along the road?

Mark one answer

- [ ] **A.**
- [ ] **B.**

- [ ] **C.**
- [ ] **D.**

Although the circle with the red border prohibits pedestrians and the other circular sign orders pedestrians and cyclists to use the path, you should look out for people ignoring these signs. Don't confuse the warning sign for a pedestrian crossing with the other triangular sign which may also have a plate showing the length of road without a footpath. See **Q552**.

Q 98 You are driving on a country road. What should you expect to see coming towards you on YOUR side of the road?

Mark one answer
- [ ] **A.** Motorcycles
- [ ] **B.** Bicycles
- [ ] **C.** Horse riders
- [ ] **D.** Pedestrians

The Highway Code tells pedestrians to walk on the right-hand side of the road when there is no pavement or footpath. This is so they see you and other oncoming traffic. They are advised to keep close to the side of the road. Cyclists and horse riders should also be on your side of the road but going in the same direction as yourself. Watch out at night for cyclists riding without lights.

Q 99 What does this sign mean?

Mark one answer
- [ ] **A.** Pedestrian crossing
- [ ] **B.** Pedestrians in the road ahead
- [ ] **C.** No pedestrians
- [ ] **D.** Route for pedestrians

Be on your guard for pedestrians who might put themselves at risk by ignoring the restriction sign.

Q 100 Your vehicle hits a pedestrian at 40mph. The pedestrian will

Mark one answer
- [ ] **A.** Certainly be killed
- [ ] **B.** Certainly survive
- [ ] **C.** Probably be killed
- [ ] **D.** Probably survive

Driving too fast is a major cause of deaths in road traffic accidents. The speed at which a car strikes a pedestrian is crucial. The few adults surviving being hit by a car travelling at 40mph would probably have severe injuries. Only about 1 in 20 pedestrians would be killed by a car travelling at 20mph. The injuries of those not killed are likely to be slight. The risk of serious injury or death is greater for children than for adults.

Q 101 You are driving behind a cyclist. You wish to turn left just ahead. You should

Mark one answer
- [ ] **A.** Overtake the cyclist before the junction
- [ ] **B.** Pull alongside the cyclist and stay level until after the junction
- [ ] **C.** Hold back until the cyclist has passed the junction
- [ ] **D.** Go around the cyclist on the junction

Think carefully before overtaking a cyclist especially if you are intending to turn left. Suppose you have to give way to pedestrians before you can turn. What happens when the cyclist you have just overtaken catches you up?

Q 102 You should NEVER attempt to overtake a cyclist

Mark one answer

- **A.** Just before you turn left
- **B.** Just before you turn right
- **C.** On a one-way street
- **D.** On a dual carriageway

A cyclist is a vulnerable road user. Cutting in front of a cyclist in order to turn left is a dangerous manoeuvre that would put the cyclist at risk. What might happen if you could not complete the turn and stopped suddenly? Always give cyclists plenty of room when overtaking on a one-way street or dual carriageway and when you are going to turn right. See **Q180**, **Q277**, **Q278**, **Q398** and **Q459**.

Q 103 When you are overtaking a cyclist you should leave as much room as you would give to a car. Why is this?

Mark one answer

- **A.** The cyclist might change lanes
- **B.** The cyclist might get off the bike
- **C.** The cyclist might swerve
- **D.** The cyclist might have to make a right turn

Two-wheeled vehicles, including mopeds and motorcycles, are less stable and more easily affected by the weather and road conditions than are cars and other vehicles on four wheels. Cycles form less than 3% of all vehicle traffic but are involved in 6% of all injury accidents.

Q 104 You are coming up to a roundabout. A cyclist is signalling to turn right. What should you do?

Mark one answer

- **A.** Overtake on the right
- **B.** Give a horn warning
- **C.** Signal the cyclist to move across
- **D.** Give the cyclist plenty of room

You may see a cyclist ahead of you but other drivers may not. Your vehicle can easily hide cyclists from the view of drivers in vehicles behind you. A cyclist turning right is in more danger than a cyclist turning left.

Q 105 You are approaching this roundabout and see the cyclist signal right. Why is the cyclist keeping to the left?

Mark one answer

- **A.** It is a quicker route for the cyclist
- **B.** The cyclist is going to turn left instead
- **C.** The cyclist thinks The Highway Code does not apply to bicycles
- **D.** The cyclist is slower and more vulnerable

Cyclists tend to keep out of danger by keeping well to the left-hand side of the road. If you are waiting at a junction, look out for cyclists in your blind spot and riding past on your left. Be particularly careful if you intend to turn left.

Q 106 You are driving behind two cyclists. They approach a roundabout in the left-hand lane. In which direction should you expect the cyclists to go?

Mark one answer

- **A.** Left
- **B.** Right
- **C.** Any direction
- **D.** Straight ahead

Remember that cyclists tend to keep well to the left especially on a roundabout and even when they are going to turn right. Cyclists should indicate their intentions but steering a cycle is more difficult when giving an arm signal.

Q 107 Which TWO should you allow extra room when overtaking?

Mark two answers

- **A.** Motorcycles
- **B.** Tractors
- **C.** Bicycles
- **D.** Road-sweeping vehicles

To overtake a moving vehicle you often have to move closer to vehicles coming towards you. Always think carefully before deciding to overtake. Give two-wheeled vehicles at least the same room as four-wheeled vehicles.

Q 108 There is a slow-moving motorcyclist ahead of you. You're unsure what the rider is going to do. You should

Mark one answer

- **A.** Pass on the left
- **B.** Pass on the right
- **C.** Stay behind
- **D.** Move closer

Give two-wheeled vehicles space. Never put motorcyclists at risk by driving too close.

Q 109 You are driving behind a moped. You want to turn left just ahead. You should

Mark one answer

- **A.** Overtake the moped before the junction
- **B.** Pull alongside the moped and stay level until just before the junction
- **C.** Sound your horn as a warning and pull in front of the moped
- **D.** Stay behind until the moped has passed the junction

A moped rider is a vulnerable road user. Cutting in front of a moped in order to turn left is a dangerous manoeuvre that would put the rider at risk. Think what might happen if you could not complete the turn and had to stop suddenly.

Q 110 You are following a motorcyclist on an uneven road. You should

Mark one answer

- **A.** Allow less room to ensure that you can be seen in their mirrors
- **B.** Overtake immediately
- **C.** Allow extra room in case they swerve to avoid pot-holes
- **D.** Allow the same room as normal because motorcyclists are not affected by road surfaces

A good motorist will try to avoid rough road surfaces and pot-holes because of the damage they can cause to tyres. Even though riders can swerve their two-wheeled vehicle at the last moment, they should try to anticipate these hazards early just as other motorists should.

Q 111 Which type of vehicle is most affected by strong winds?

Mark one answer
- **A.** Tractor
- **B.** Motorcycle
- **C.** Car
- **D.** Tanker

Q 112 Why should you allow extra room when overtaking a motorcyclist on a windy day?

Mark one answer
- **A.** The rider may turn off suddenly to get out of the wind
- **B.** The rider may be blown across in front of you
- **C.** The rider may stop suddenly
- **D.** The rider may be travelling faster than normal

The weather and road conditions affect two-wheeled vehicles far more than four-wheeled vehicles. When you are alongside a motorcycle, your car may screen it from the wind. So when you and other vehicles are overtaking the motorcycle, the rider may have to cope with being blown off course by strong gusts of wind.

Q 113 Motorcycle riders are vulnerable because they

Mark one answer
- **A.** Are easy for other road users to see
- **B.** Are difficult for other road users to see
- **C.** Are likely to have breakdowns
- **D.** Cannot give arm signals

Riders may avoid delays by weaving their two-wheeled vehicles through traffic queues. Motorists should always check their blind spots, especially for moped riders and motorcyclists who are able to move faster than pedal cyclists.

Q 114 Motorcyclists should wear bright clothing mainly because

Mark one answer
- **A.** They must do so by law
- **B.** It helps keep them cool in summer
- **C.** The colours are popular
- **D.** Drivers often do not see them

In overcast weather motorcycle riders may be difficult to spot if they are wearing black protective clothing. Some motorcyclists draw attention to their presence by riding with dipped headlights switched on even in daylight. See **Q119** and **Q120**.

Q 115 Where should you take **particular** care to look out for motorcyclists and cyclists?

Mark one answer
- **A.** On dual carriageways
- **B.** At junctions
- **C.** At zebra crossings
- **D.** On one-way streets

Two-wheeled vehicles are smaller and more difficult to see than most four-wheeled vehicles. Consequently it is easy not to notice a cyclist, moped rider or even a motorcyclist hidden in one of your blind spots. Always check for them especially if you intend to turn left.

Q 116 Where in particular should you look out for motorcyclists?

Mark one answer

- [ ] **A.** In a filling station
- [ ] **B.** At a road junction
- [ ] **C.** Near a service area
- [ ] **D.** When entering a car park

Always look out for mopeds and motorcycles wherever you are. These two-wheeled vehicles can appear suddenly from nowhere. They have a habit of appearing in the wrong place just as you are turning into or out of a major road.

Q 117 When emerging from a side road into a queue of traffic which vehicles can be especially difficult to see?

Mark one answer

- [ ] **A.** Motorcycles
- [ ] **B.** Tractors
- [ ] **C.** Milk floats
- [ ] **D.** Cars

In heavy traffic motorcyclists and moped riders may jump the queues by overtaking in spite of the risks from vehicles coming from the opposite direction. They could be hidden from the view of other road users even when overtaking a small car.

Q 118 You are waiting to come out of a side road. Why should you watch carefully for motorcycles?

Mark one answer

- [ ] **A.** Motorcycles are usually faster than cars
- [ ] **B.** Police patrols often use motorcycles
- [ ] **C.** Motorcycles are small and hard to see
- [ ] **D.** Motorcycles have right of way

Cars parked along a major road can make life very difficult for traffic turning out of side roads. Always look for two-wheeled vehicles that may be approaching along the major road but are hidden from your view by other traffic or parked vehicles.

Q 119 In daylight, an approaching motorcyclist is using a dipped headlight. Why?

Mark one answer

- [ ] **A.** So that the rider can be seen more easily
- [ ] **B.** To stop the battery over-charging
- [ ] **C.** To improve the rider's vision
- [ ] **D.** The rider is inviting you to proceed

Q 120 Motorcyclists ride in daylight with their headlights switched on because

Mark one answer

- [ ] **A.** It is a legal requirement
- [ ] **B.** There's a speed trap ahead
- [ ] **C.** They need to be seen
- [ ] **D.** There are speed humps ahead

When the weather is overcast and daylight is poor, we should use dipped headlights to alert other road users of our presence. However, we should take care not to dazzle other drivers by using our headlights on full beam.

Q 121 You notice horse riders in front. What should you do FIRST?

Remember that horses and riders must obey the rules of the road by travelling in the same direction as other traffic on the same side of the road. Look for other clues like fresh dung on the road to warn you of horses or other animals ahead.

Q 123 As you are driving along you meet a group of horses and riders from a riding school. Why should you be extra cautious?

Mark one answer
- **A.** They will be moving in single file
- **B.** They will be moving slowly
- **C.** Many of the riders may be learners
- **D.** The horses will panic more because they are in a group

Mark one answer
- **A.** Pull out to the middle of the road
- **B.** Be prepared to slow down
- **C.** Accelerate around them
- **D.** Signal right

Take extra care near horse riders. Slow down. Give them plenty of room. Make eye contact with the riders if possible. Drive smoothly and quietly to reduce the risk of making the horses panic and upsetting their riders. Horse and rider are both vulnerable road users.

Look for the road sign warning of accompanied horses or ponies. This is usually found near riding stables and bridle paths. Remember that riders under 14 years of age must, by law, wear a suitable protective riding helmet.

Q 124 How should you overtake horse riders?

Mark one answer
- **A.** Drive up close and overtake as soon as possible
- **B.** Speed is not important but allow plenty of room
- **C.** Use your horn just once to warn them
- **D.** Drive slowly and leave plenty of room

Q 122 You are driving on a narrow country road. Where would you find it most difficult to see horses and riders ahead of you?

Mark one answer
- **A.** On left-hand bends
- **B.** When travelling downhill
- **C.** When travelling uphill
- **D.** On right-hand bends

Horses may panic and shy at sudden movements and sounds. Always give horse riders a wide berth. Make eye contact with the riders if you can. Drive by slowly, smoothly and as quietly as possible. Do not flash your lights or sound your horn. See **Q269**, **Q270** and **Q595**.

Q 125 A horse rider is in the left-hand lane approaching a roundabout. The driver behind should expect the rider to

Mark one answer
- [ ] **A.** Go in any direction
- [ ] **B.** Turn right
- [ ] **C.** Turn left
- [ ] **D.** Go ahead

Horse riders and cyclists should try to keep as far away as possible from other traffic. Be patient and expect them to stay to your left even if they give an arm signal to turn right at a junction or a roundabout. The Highway Code tells horse riders to keep left when they are riding, to keep the horse to their left when they are leading it and to avoid roundabouts wherever possible. The Highway Code tells horse riders using a roundabout to keep left but to signal right when riding across exits to show they are not leaving. Horse riders should signal left just before they leave the roundabout.

Q 126 Which THREE should you do when passing sheep on a road?

Mark three answers
- [ ] **A.** Allow plenty of room
- [ ] **B.** Drive very slowly
- [ ] **C.** Pass quickly but quietly
- [ ] **D.** Briefly sound your horn
- [ ] **E.** Be ready to stop

Remember that when passing animals you should drive slowly in a lower gear. Loud noises startle animals. Sheep are nervous animals, easily frightened by noise and sudden movement. Sheep can easily injure themselves if they bolt. If your vehicle injures a stray sheep on the road, you must report the incident to the police within 24 hours if you cannot give your name and address to the sheep's owner. See **Q269**, **Q270** and **Q595**.

Q 127 What's the most common factor in causing road accidents?

Mark one answer
- [ ] **A.** Weather conditions
- [ ] **B.** Driver error
- [ ] **C.** Road conditions
- [ ] **D.** Mechanical failure

95% of all road traffic accidents involve an element of human error. 65% are caused by human factors alone. Fewer than 5% of accidents are caused solely by road conditions or by vehicle defects. Faulty tyres and brakes contribute more than mechanical defects.

Q 128 Which of the following are a major cause of motorcycle collisions?

Mark one answer
- [ ] **A.** Car drivers
- [ ] **B.** Moped riders
- [ ] **C.** Sunny weather conditions
- [ ] **D.** Traffic lights

Mopeds and motorcycles are easily hidden from a car driver's view. As part of your MSM–PSL routine, make sure you check your blind spots before changing speed and/or direction.

Q 129 You have just passed your driving test. How likely are you to have an accident, compared with other drivers?

Mark one answer
- [ ] **A.** More likely
- [ ] **B.** It depends on your age
- [ ] **C.** Less likely
- [ ] **D.** About the same

There is no substitute for experience. But practice makes perfect only if you practise the correct techniques and develop the attitudes of the good defensive driver.

Q 130 How would you react to other drivers who appear to be inexperienced?

Mark one answer

- **A.** Sound your horn to warn them of your presence
- **B.** Be patient and prepared for them to react more slowly
- **C.** Flash your headlights to indicate that it's safe for them to proceed
- **D.** Overtake them as soon as possible

In an emergency you should flash your headlights and/or sound your horn to warn others of your presence and possible danger. Do not create a dangerous situation by being impatient and overtaking before it is safe to do so. Good defensive drivers are always tolerant of others.

Q 131 Which age group is most likely to be involved in a road accident?

Mark one answer

- **A.** 36 to 45-year-olds
- **B.** 55-year-olds and over
- **C.** 46 to 55-year-olds
- **D.** 17 to 25-year-olds

About 16% of all drivers and riders are aged between 17 and 25. But of all drivers and riders involved in injury accidents, about 32% are aged between 17 and 25. Young, inexperienced drivers under the age of 25 are twice as likely to be involved in accidents compared to older, more experienced drivers.

Q 132 You are following a car driven by an elderly driver. You should

Mark one answer

- **A.** Expect the driver to drive badly
- **B.** Flash your lights and overtake
- **C.** Be aware that the driver's reactions may not be as fast as yours
- **D.** Stay close behind and drive carefully

Close following, headlight flashing and unnecessary overtaking are signs of aggressive driving. A licence grants the holder the privilege of driving on the public roads. You could lose your licence for careless, dangerous or inconsiderate driving. See **Q160–163** and **Q587**.

Q 133 As a new driver, how can you decrease your risk of accidents on the motorway?

Mark one answer

- **A.** By keeping up with the car in front
- **B.** By never driving over 45mph
- **C.** By driving only in the nearside lane
- **D.** By taking further training

New learner drivers are not allowed to drive on the motorway. Newly qualified drivers are. Experience on some dual carriageways will help to prepare you for motorway driving. But there is no substitute for motorway tuition and practice under the guidance of an approved driving instructor.

Q 134 You want to turn right from a junction but your view is restricted by parked vehicles. What should you do?

Mark one answer

- **A.** Move out quickly, but be prepared to stop
- **B.** Sound your horn and pull out if there is no reply
- **C.** Stop, then move slowly forward until you have a clear view
- **D.** Stop, get out and look along the main road to check

When parked cars obstruct your view you have no choice but to 'feel your way' forward until you can be sure it is safe to turn. Remember this and think of other road users when you are choosing a safe and convenient place to park your vehicle. See **Q269**, **Q270** and **Q595**.

Q 135 At road junctions which of the following are most vulnerable?

Mark three answers

- **A.** Cyclists
- **B.** Motorcyclists
- **C.** Pedestrians
- **D.** Car drivers
- **E.** Lorry drivers

Human error is the cause of most accidents. A high proportion of all accidents happen at junctions. Many involve pedestrians and other vulnerable road users who are at risk because the drivers of other vehicles do not see them in time.

Q 136 The approach to a zebra crossing is marked with zigzag lines. Which TWO must you NOT do within the marked area?

Mark two answers

- **A.** Overtake
- **B.** Cross the lines
- **C.** Drive at more than 10mph
- **D.** Park

You may exceed 10mph and drive over the zigzag lines if the crossing is clear of pedestrians and you are not overtaking. Always approach crossings with care; within the area marked by the zigzag lines never park or stop, even to pick up or set down a disabled passenger. See **Q137**, **Q380** and **Q599**.

Q 137 When may you stop on a pedestrian crossing?

Mark one answer

- **A.** Not at any time
- **B.** To avoid an accident
- **C.** When there's a queue of traffic in front of you
- **D.** Between the hours of 11pm and 7am

You may stop in front of or behind a crossing within the area marked by the zigzag lines. You must stop to give precedence to pedestrians, to obey pelican crossing lights or the signals from an authorised person and to avoid an accident. But you must **not** stop on the crossing itself. See **Q136** above.

Q 138 In which THREE places would parking your vehicle cause danger or obstruction to other road users?

Mark three answers

- [ ] **A.** In front of a property entrance
- [ ] **B.** At or near a bus stop
- [ ] **C.** On your driveway
- [ ] **D.** In a marked parking space
- [ ] **E.** On the approach to a level crossing

> It is an offence to cause unnecessary obstruction. It is a separate offence to leave your vehicle in a dangerous position. Where possible use an authorised parking bay or your own driveway. See **Q495**.

Q 139 You are driving towards a zebra crossing. Pedestrians are waiting to cross. You should

Mark one answer

- [ ] **A.** Give way to the elderly and infirm only
- [ ] **B.** Slow down and prepare to stop
- [ ] **C.** Use your headlamps to indicate they can cross
- [ ] **D.** Wave at them to cross the road

> Always approach zebra crossings with caution. Look for pedestrians waiting to cross. At zebra crossings, pedestrians have absolute priority to cross once they have placed a foot on the crossing. Give pedestrians, especially the elderly and infirm, time to cross when they are on the crossing. You should treat a zebra crossing with an island as two separate crossings. But beware that pedestrians may be treating it as one crossing.

Q 140 You have stopped at a pedestrian crossing. To allow pedestrians to cross you should

Mark one answer

- [ ] **A.** Wait until they have crossed
- [ ] **B.** Edge your vehicle forward slowly
- [ ] **C.** Wait, revving your engine
- [ ] **D.** Signal to pedestrians to cross

Q 141 You stop for pedestrians waiting to cross at a zebra crossing. They do not start to cross. What should you do?

Mark one answer

- [ ] **A.** Be patient and wait
- [ ] **B.** Sound your horn
- [ ] **C.** Drive on
- [ ] **D.** Wave them to cross

> You normally do not need to stop for pedestrians waiting at a zebra crossing. If you do stop to let them cross, make eye contact, smile and be patient. Remember that you must not sound your horn when stationary except in an emergency. And it is dangerous to wave pedestrians into the road in case they do so without checking that it is safe. See **Q269**, **Q270** and **Q595**.

Q 142 When should you beckon pedestrians to cross the road?

Mark one answer

- [ ] **A.** At pedestrian crossings
- [ ] **B.** At no time
- [ ] **C.** At junctions
- [ ] **D.** At school crossings

> Pedestrians waiting to cross a road must check for themselves that it is safe. Only uniformed police officers and traffic wardens have the authority to control pedestrian traffic. If you beckon them on, you might just wave them into the path of another vehicle. See **Q594**.

Q 143 A pelican crossing that crosses the road in a STRAIGHT line and has a central island MUST be treated as

Mark one answer
- [ ] **A.** One crossing in daylight only
- [ ] **B.** One complete crossing
- [ ] **C.** Two separate crossings
- [ ] **D.** Two crossings during darkness

> If a pelican crossing connects to two **different** parts of a central island and does **not** cross the road in a straight line, you treat this staggered crossing as two separate pelican crossings even if both sets of lights are synchronised.

Q 144 You are approaching a pelican crossing. The amber light is flashing. You must

Mark one answer
- [ ] **A.** Give way to pedestrians who are crossing
- [ ] **B.** Encourage pedestrians to cross
- [ ] **C.** Not move until the green light appears
- [ ] **D.** Stop even if the crossing is clear

> At pelican crossings pedestrians see the green man flashing at the same time as drivers see the amber lights flashing. This tells pedestrians they should not start to cross but they will have time to finish safely if they have already started to cross. You may drive on if the crossing is clear of pedestrians even if the amber light is flashing. Always look for the pedestrian dashing across against the flashing green man.

Q 145 What must a driver do at a pelican crossing when the amber light is flashing?

Mark one answer
- [ ] **A.** Signal the pedestrian to cross
- [ ] **B.** Always wait for the green light before proceeding
- [ ] **C.** Give way to any pedestrians on the crossing
- [ ] **D.** Wait for the red-and-amber light before proceeding

> You should think of a PEdestrian LIght-CONtrolled crossing as a footpath over the road, and allow any pedestrians on the crossing to finish walking across the road even if the flashing amber lights have changed to green.

Q 146 At a pelican crossing the flashing amber light means you should

Mark one answer
- [ ] **A.** Stop, if you can do so safely
- [ ] **B.** Give way to pedestrians already on the crossing
- [ ] **C.** Stop and wait for the green light
- [ ] **D.** Give way to pedestrians waiting to cross

> If the amber light is flashing and pedestrians are crossing, you must stop. It may be safe for you to continue if the pedestrians are out of danger on the other side of the road and moving away from you. Always give way and wait if there is any doubt.

Q 147 At toucan crossings

Mark two answers
- [ ] **A.** There is no flashing amber light
- [ ] **B.** Cyclists are not permitted
- [ ] **C.** There is a continuously flashing amber beacon
- [ ] **D.** Pedestrians and cyclists may cross
- [ ] **E.** You only stop if someone is waiting to cross

Red lights order traffic to stop when pedestrians and cyclists are using the crossing. The lights turn green when the crossing is clear and traffic is allowed to go.

Q 148 What type of crossing is this?

Mark one answer

A. A zebra crossing
B. A pelican crossing
C. A puffin crossing
D. A toucan crossing

At pelican, puffin and zebra crossings, cyclists should dismount and push their bicycles across the road. Watch out for those cyclists, usually children, who seem unaware of this rule.

Q 149 At toucan crossings, apart from pedestrians you should be aware of

Mark one answer

A. Emergency vehicles emerging
B. Buses pulling out
C. Trams crossing in front
D. Cyclists riding across

Q 150 Who can use a toucan crossing?

Mark two answers

A. Trains
B. Cyclists
C. Buses
D. Pedestrians
E. Trams

These crossings often connect paths on either side of the road which should be shared and used by pedestrians and cyclists.

Q 151 Which vehicles are normally fitted with amber flashing beacons on the roof?

Mark two answers

A. Doctor's car
B. Bomb disposal team
C. Blood transfusion team
D. Breakdown recovery vehicles
E. Coastguard
F. Maintenance vehicles

Amber lights signal danger and usually flash. They are used on highway maintenance vehicles and at road works. Flashing amber is used on motorways, at pelican crossings, on some school crossing signs and at zebra crossings.

Q 152 What type of emergency vehicle is fitted with a green flashing light?

Mark one answer

A. Fire engine
B. Road gritter
C. Ambulance
D. Doctor's car

Q 153 A flashing green beacon on a vehicle means

Mark one answer
- [ ] **A.** Police on non-urgent duties
- [ ] **B.** Doctor on an emergency call
- [ ] **C.** Road safety patrol operating
- [ ] **D.** Gritting in progress

> Flashing blue lights are used by the police and on ambulances, fire engines and other emergency vehicles. Doctors responding to an emergency call use a flashing green light.

Q 154 A vehicle has a flashing green light. What does this mean?

Mark one answer
- [ ] **A.** A doctor is answering an emergency call
- [ ] **B.** The vehicle is slow-moving
- [ ] **C.** It is a motorway police patrol vehicle
- [ ] **D.** A vehicle is carrying hazardous chemicals

> Vehicles transporting hazardous chemicals do not display flashing lights but they usually carry panels displaying special hazard symbols and information about the chemicals.

Q 155 Which THREE of the following emergency vehicles will use blue flashing beacons?

Mark three answers
- [ ] **A.** Motorway maintenance
- [ ] **B.** Bomb disposal team
- [ ] **C.** Blood transfusion
- [ ] **D.** Police vehicle
- [ ] **E.** Breakdown recovery vehicle

> A flashing blue light, often accompanied by a siren, is a warning to road users to pull over and clear the way for emergency vehicles to drive through as quickly as possible.

Q 156 Which THREE of these emergency services might have blue flashing beacons?

Mark three answers
- [ ] **A.** Coastguard
- [ ] **B.** Bomb disposal team
- [ ] **C.** Gritting lorries
- [ ] **D.** Animal ambulances
- [ ] **E.** Mountain rescue
- [ ] **F.** Doctors' cars

> Doctors on an emergency call may display a flashing green light on their car. Gritting lorries, motorway maintenance and breakdown recovery vehicles display flashing amber lights.

Q 157 A two-second gap between yourself and the car in front is sufficient when conditions are

Mark one answer
- [ ] **A.** Wet
- [ ] **B.** Good
- [ ] **C.** Damp
- [ ] **D.** Foggy

> The Highway Code golden rule is: drive at a speed that allows you to stop well within the distance you can see to be clear. If you are following another vehicle, leave enough space so that you can pull up safely if the vehicle in front suddenly slows down or stops. See **Q304**.

Q 158 You are following a vehicle on a wet road. You should leave a time gap of at least

Mark one answer

- [ ] **A.** One second
- [ ] **B.** Two seconds
- [ ] **C.** Three seconds
- [ ] **D.** Four seconds

To be safe, you should not be closer than your overall stopping distance. This distance is not a target. You should increase it in wet weather. You could use this rhyme: 'Only a fool breaks the two-second rule. And say it again when driving in rain'. See **Q304**.

Q 159 What should you use your horn for?

Mark one answer

- [ ] **A.** To alert others to your presence
- [ ] **B.** To claim your right of way
- [ ] **C.** To greet other road users
- [ ] **D.** To signal your annoyance

The horn is an **emergency** signal. It distracts other road users if you make them look for danger. Never use your horn between 11.30pm and 7.00am in a built-up area. Never use it when stationary unless there is danger from a moving vehicle. Think about deaf road users. See **Q269**, **Q270** and **Q595**.

Q 160 You think the driver of the vehicle in front has forgotten to cancel his right indicator. You should

Mark one answer

- [ ] **A.** Sound your horn before overtaking
- [ ] **B.** Overtake on the left if there's room
- [ ] **C.** Flash your lights to alert the driver
- [ ] **D.** Stay behind and not overtake

You should give the driver plenty of room in case he or she is looking out for a junction and makes a sudden turn.

Q 161 A vehicle pulls out in front of you at a junction. What should you do?

Mark one answer

- [ ] **A.** Swerve past it and blow your horn
- [ ] **B.** Flash your headlights and drive up close behind
- [ ] **C.** Slow down and be ready to stop
- [ ] **D.** Accelerate past it immediately

Don't respond to inconsiderate road users by being inconsiderate yourself. What appears to be inconsiderate behaviour could simply be the actions of a new and inexperienced road user. Drivers should try to remember what it felt like to be a learner driver and a novice. See **Q587** and **Q595**.

Q 162 You should ONLY flash your headlamps to other road users

Mark one answer

- [ ] **A.** To show that you are giving way
- [ ] **B.** To show that you are about to reverse
- [ ] **C.** To tell them that you have right of way
- [ ] **D.** To let them know that you're there

What is the effect of seeing flashing headlights? The headlights have drawn your attention to the vehicle's presence. What else can you be sure of? Only one thing – the driver's headlights work! See **Q587**.

Q 163 You are driving at the legal speed limit. A vehicle comes up quickly behind, flashing its headlamps. You should

Mark one answer

- **A.** Accelerate to maintain a gap behind you
- **B.** Touch the brakes to show your brake lights
- **C.** Maintain your speed and prevent the vehicle from overtaking
- **D.** Allow the vehicle to overtake

Good drivers prefer to have bad drivers in front so they can see them and keep away from them. The only way you should influence bad drivers is by setting them a good example that they can copy. Defensive drivers do **not** respond to aggressive drivers by being aggressive themselves.

Q 164 You are in a line of traffic. The driver behind you is following very closely. What action should you take?

Mark one answer

- **A.** Slow down, gradually increasing the gap between you and the vehicle in front
- **B.** Ignore the following driver and continue to drive within the speed limit
- **C.** Signal left and wave the following driver past
- **D.** Move out wider to a position just left of the road's centre line

You can control your distance from the vehicle in front of you but you cannot control your distance from the vehicle behind you. If a vehicle is following you too closely, be prepared to give the driver every opportunity to overtake you safely and get out of your way.

Q 165 You are driving at the legal speed limit. A vehicle behind wants to overtake. Should you try to prevent the driver overtaking?

Mark one answer

- **A.** No, unless it's safe to do so
- **B.** Yes, because the other driver is acting dangerously
- **C.** No, not at any time
- **D.** Yes, because the other driver is breaking the law

Overtaking is an extremely dangerous manoeuvre at the best of times. Never do anything to frustrate another road user and risk making the situation worse. Can you ever know why other drivers drive the way they do? A driver may be rushing a casualty to hospital. Set other drivers a good example of defensive driving but leave them to decide whether or not to copy you. You cannot make other drivers keep within the law. If you try you may end up breaking the law yourself and causing a serious accident.

Q 166 You are driving in traffic at the speed limit for the road. The driver behind is trying to overtake. You should

Mark one answer

- **A.** Move closer to the car ahead, so the driver behind has no room to overtake
- **B.** Wave the driver behind to overtake when it is safe
- **C.** Keep a steady course and allow the driver behind to overtake
- **D.** Accelerate to get away from the driver behind

Be considerate of other road users, however foolish they may seem. Good defensive drivers stay within the law and do their best to keep themselves and other road users out of danger. Drive so that you can see and be seen by others. Make your intentions clear so that other road users can decide for themselves their safest course of action.

Q 167 A long, heavily loaded lorry is taking a long time to overtake you. What should you do?

Mark one answer
- **A.** Speed up
- **B.** Slow down
- **C.** Hold your speed
- **D.** Change direction

Try to avoid thinking that you are competing in a race with other drivers and their vehicles for road space. Racing on the public highway is a serious offence.

Q 168 There is a tractor ahead of you. You wish to overtake but you are NOT sure if it is safe to do so. You should

Mark one answer
- **A.** Follow another overtaking vehicle through
- **B.** Sound your horn to the slow vehicle to pull over
- **C.** Speed through but flash your lights to oncoming traffic
- **D.** Not overtake if you are in doubt

Before we overtake we should be really sure that it is necessary and safe. Remember how quickly the gap can close between vehicles approaching each other from opposite directions. See **Q20**.

Q 169 You are driving a slow-moving vehicle on a narrow road. When traffic wishes to overtake you should

Mark one answer
- **A.** Take no action
- **B.** Put your hazard warning lights on
- **C.** Stop immediately and wave them on
- **D.** Pull in safely as soon as you can do so

Q 170 You are driving a slow-moving vehicle on a narrow winding road. You should

Mark one answer
- **A.** Keep well out to stop vehicles overtaking dangerously
- **B.** Wave following vehicles past you if you think they can overtake quickly
- **C.** Pull in safely when you can, to let following vehicles overtake
- **D.** Give a left signal when it is safe for vehicles to overtake you

Try never to hold up traffic by driving unnecessarily slowly. If your vehicle is a slow-moving tractor or agricultural vehicle, be considerate and let faster-moving traffic pass where possible. But leave the decision to overtake to the drivers. Do not wave them on even though the road ahead may seem safe to you. Never signal except to indicate that you are going to stop or turn.

Q 171 You are in a one-way street and want to turn right. You should position yourself

Mark one answer

- [ ] **A.** In the right-hand lane
- [ ] **B.** In the left-hand lane
- [ ] **C.** In either lane, depending on the traffic
- [ ] **D.** Just left of the centre line

One-way streets are to help keep traffic flowing freely. You may overtake on the left or the right but you must watch for pedestrians looking the wrong way while crossing a one-way street. Unless road markings or traffic signs indicate otherwise, the left-hand lane is for going left, the right-hand lane is for going right and the most appropriate lane according to the circumstances for going straight ahead. Choose the correct lane for your exit as soon as you can. Never change lanes suddenly.

Q 172 A bus is stopped at a bus stop ahead of you. Its right-hand indicator is flashing. You should

Mark one answer

- [ ] **A.** Flash your headlights and slow down
- [ ] **B.** Slow down and give way if it is safe to do so
- [ ] **C.** Sound your horn and keep going
- [ ] **D.** Slow down and then sound your horn

Bus drivers must try to keep to their timetable. You can help them. Remember that their large vehicles are often difficult to manoeuvre and their vision to their rear may be poor. Always drive to see and be seen. Use your horn and flash your lights only in an emergency. See **Q269**, **Q270**, **Q587** and **Q595**.

The three topics in this section are about your vehicle. The first is concerned with the factors affecting how your vehicle responds to your controls. The second topic explains the regulations about loading your vehicle. The third is about detecting faults that could affect your vehicle's performance and make it unsafe, and also covers safety equipment.

VEHICLE HANDLING

Good drivers match how they drive to suit their vehicle and the conditions. You must know and understand what effect road and weather conditions can have upon safe speeds, braking and following distances. Saying the rhyme 'Only a fool breaks the two-second rule' will not give you the minimum following distance on wet or icy roads. You must also know and understand what effect the time of day and the lighting conditions could have on your driving.

VEHICLE LOADING

You need to know that it is an offence to carry in your vehicle more adult passengers than there are seats. And it can be an offence to let children sit on adult laps.

If something on your roof rack overhangs your vehicle by more than 2m (6½ft), you must make it obvious to other road users by attaching a projection triangle or a red cloth to the overhanging end of the load. You should also know that a heavily loaded roof rack will make your vehicle less stable and less safe. It is an offence to load your vehicle so that the load exceeds the maximum gross weight or axle weight of your vehicle.

SAFETY AND YOUR VEHICLE

Good drivers develop 'car sympathy'. They drive defensively with care and consideration for their own vehicle as well as for other road users. You should become used to the way your vehicle handles and sounds. This will help you to recognise the warning signs of a fault early enough to prevent serious damage or mechanical breakdown occurring.

By law, the condition of your vehicle must not constitute a danger of injury to yourself or others. It is an absolute offence to use a vehicle breaching the Construction and Use Regulations (CUR) even if you are unaware of the vehicle's fault. The regulations that require you to keep all the different parts of your vehicle in good working order are listed in The Highway Code (in the section on the road user and the law). For a motor car over three years old, there are specific parts that must pass the Department of Transport test for the car to receive its MOT Certificate. These parts include brakes, steering and suspension, tyres and wheels, exhaust, indicators, lights and reflectors, windscreens and washers, windows, seat belts and fittings, speedometer and horn.

Seat belts can save lives and lessen injuries. If seat belts are fitted, you and your passengers must wear them. The driver is responsible for passengers under 14 years of age. Children under 3 years old must wear an appropriate child restraint. Head restraints help to prevent serious neck injuries when the vehicle is struck from behind. An airbag fitted in the steering wheel inflates instantly to form a cushion between the driver and the steering wheel when the vehicle has a head-on collision. A red triangle to warn other traffic of a hazard should be placed before the hazard and at least 50m (164ft) on ordinary roads or 150m (492ft) on the motorway hard shoulder. You should know what extinguisher to use in the event of a fire.

Accelerating too quickly, high-speed driving in low gears and harsh braking will create noise, waste fuel and wear out tyres unnecessarily. If you drive a vehicle with a faulty silencer and exhaust system, you are committing an offence as well as causing excessive noise and atmospheric pollution. The horn is to warn others of your presence or danger. It is an offence to sound it when stationary or when driving in a built-up area between 11.30pm and 7am. It is also an offence to drive your car if the horn does not work.

Q 173 You should not drive with your foot on the clutch for longer than necessary because it

Mark one answer

- **A.** Increases wear on the gearbox
- **B.** Increases petrol consumption
- **C.** Reduces your control of the vehicle
- **D.** Reduces the grip of the tyres

You press down the clutch pedal when changing gear and just before stopping. Your vehicle will usually slow down when you take your foot off the accelerator pedal. The engine can act as a brake when in gear but not when out of gear.

Q 174 Why is pressing the clutch down for long periods a bad habit?

Mark one answer

- **A.** It reduces the car's speed when going downhill
- **B.** It causes the engine to wear out more quickly
- **C.** It reduces the driver's control of the vehicle
- **D.** It causes the engine to use more fuel

When your clutch is down your vehicle is out of gear and your engine cannot help to reduce your speed. See **Q178**.

Q 175 You should avoid 'coasting' your vehicle because it could

Mark one answer

- **A.** Damage the suspension
- **B.** Increase tyre wear
- **C.** Flatten the battery
- **D.** Reduce steering control

A vehicle's battery will normally be charging whenever the engine is running. A panel warning light will usually tell you if the charging circuit has developed an electrical fault.

Q 176 Coasting the vehicle

Mark one answer

- **A.** Improves the driver's control
- **B.** Makes steering easier
- **C.** Reduces the driver's control
- **D.** Uses more fuel

Use just the right amount of acceleration and the correct gear to negotiate bends and corners safely. Drive with the engine just pulling the vehicle around the curve. Do not use too much acceleration. Remember – the lower the gear the more control you have.

Q 177 Why is coasting wrong?

Mark one answer

- **A.** It will cause the car to skid
- **B.** It will make the engine stall
- **C.** The engine will run faster
- **D.** There is no engine braking

Applying the brakes is the only way to stop your vehicle when it is out of gear. Never drive with your foot resting on the clutch pedal. You could wear out your clutch. Plan ahead so you always have plenty of time to put your foot on to the clutch pedal.

Q 178 What are TWO main reasons why coasting downhill is wrong?

Mark two answers

- **A.** Petrol consumption will be higher
- **B.** The vehicle will pick up speed
- **C.** It puts more wear and tear on the tyres
- **D.** You have less braking and steering control
- **E.** It damages the engine

Going down steep hills you are advised to keep in low gear so the engine can help the brakes to control your speed. Rolling downhill out of gear is too dangerous to justify the small saving in petrol consumption.

Q 179 When driving a car fitted with automatic transmission what would you use 'kick down' for?

Mark one answer

- **A.** Cruise control
- **B.** Quick acceleration
- **C.** Slow braking
- **D.** Fuel economy

Good drivers will often change down to a lower gear to increase acceleration, especially when overtaking. You can select a lower gear in an automatic vehicle by kicking down sharply on the accelerator pedal.

Q 180 In which THREE of these situations may you overtake another vehicle on the left?

Mark three answers

- **A.** When you are in a one-way street
- **B.** When approaching a motorway slip road where you will be turning off
- **C.** When the vehicle in front is signalling to turn right
- **D.** When a slower vehicle is travelling in the right-hand lane of a dual carriageway
- **E.** In slow-moving traffic queues when traffic in the right-hand lane is moving more slowly

In general you should not overtake on the left. You may do so in a one-way street, but make sure it is safe and watch for traffic moving across from the right-hand side of the street. When overtaking a vehicle which is signalling right, watch for traffic that may be hidden by it. See **Q277**, **Q278**, **Q398** and **Q459**.

Q 181 You wish to overtake on a dual carriageway. You see in your mirror that the car behind has pulled out to overtake you. You should

Mark one answer

- **A.** Not signal until the car has passed
- **B.** Signal and pull out to overtake
- **C.** Signal to tell the driver behind that you also want to overtake
- **D.** Touch the brakes to show your brake lights

The repeating cycle of LAD–MSM–PSL is the basic routine of good driving. You Look in your mirrors to Assess the actions of following traffic in order to Decide what you should do next. You use your Mirrors before deciding to Signal your intention to begin a Manœuvre. Avoid any change in your speed and/or direction that would cause another road user to change their speed and/or direction.

Q 182 > You are driving in the left-hand lane of a dual carriageway. Another vehicle overtakes and pulls in front of you leaving you without enough separation distance. You should

Mark one answer
- [ ] **A.** Move to the right lane
- [ ] **B.** Continue as you are
- [ ] **C.** Drop back
- [ ] **D.** Sound your horn

Always keep a safe gap between your vehicle and the one in front. The higher the speed the greater the gap. Use the two-second rule. If the gap is less than your overall stopping distance you are taking a risk. When you have overtaken another vehicle, move back smoothly and quickly but do not reduce the gap from the vehicle behind by cutting back in too soon. See **Q269**, **Q270** and **Q595**.

Q 183 > You see a vehicle coming towards you on a single-track road. You should

Mark one answer
- [ ] **A.** Stop at a passing place
- [ ] **B.** Reverse back to the main road
- [ ] **C.** Do an emergency stop
- [ ] **D.** Put on your hazard flashers

Single-track roads usually have places where vehicles may pass one another. If the passing place is on your left you pull into it. If the passing place is on your right you pull up opposite it. Do not treat a passing place as a lay-by. See **Q185** and **Q433**.

Q 184 > You are driving downhill. There is a car parked on the other side of the road. Large, slow lorries are coming towards you. You should

Mark one answer
- [ ] **A.** Keep going because you have the right of way
- [ ] **B.** Slow down and give way
- [ ] **C.** Speed up and get past quickly
- [ ] **D.** Pull over on the right behind the parked car

Parked cars often reduce the effective width of a road to a single carriageway. So we should always think carefully before parking on the road. Good defensive drivers follow the rule of giving way to uphill traffic.

Q 185 > Which TWO are correct? The passing places on a single-track road are

Mark two answers
- [ ] **A.** For taking a rest from driving
- [ ] **B.** To pull into if an oncoming vehicle wants to proceed
- [ ] **C.** For stopping and checking your route
- [ ] **D.** To turn the car around in, if you are lost
- [ ] **E.** To pull into if the car behind wants to overtake

Be prepared to reverse back to a passing place if you encounter an oncoming vehicle on a single-track road, especially if the place behind is nearer than the one ahead. A small vehicle should normally give way to a larger vehicle. Downhill traffic should give way to uphill traffic. See **Q183** and **Q433**.

Q 186 Which THREE of the following will affect your stopping distance?

Mark three answers
- **A.** How fast you are going
- **B.** The tyres on your vehicle
- **C.** The time of day
- **D.** The weather
- **E.** The street lighting

At 30mph in perfect road conditions the minimum overall stopping distance for an alert driver is 23m (75ft). At 60mph the minimum overall stopping distance is 73m (240ft). If you double your speed you will at least treble your stopping distance. If the road becomes wet your stopping distance is at least doubled. And your stopping distance will be even greater if your tyres are in poor condition.

Q 187 You are driving in heavy rain. Your steering suddenly becomes very light. You should

Mark one answer
- **A.** Steer towards the side of the road
- **B.** Apply gentle acceleration
- **C.** Brake firmly to reduce speed
- **D.** Ease off the accelerator

If your steering becomes very light you should consider this as advance warning of possible danger. Your first action must be to take your foot off the accelerator pedal. Braking or steering will have no effect until the tyres grip the road surface. Do not rely on ABS (anti-lock brake system) to solve this situation.

Q 188 How can you best control your vehicle when driving in snow?

Mark one answer
- **A.** By driving slowly in as high a gear as possible
- **B.** By staying in low gear and gripping the steering wheel tightly
- **C.** By driving in first gear
- **D.** By keeping the engine revs high and slipping the clutch

If possible DO NOT DRIVE IN SNOW. Stay indoors. Heavy snow falling on ice-covered roads may be the worst weather conditions facing drivers. If you are caught in a snow storm, you should abandon your vehicle only as a last resort. Keep to main roads, follow other vehicles' tyre tracks and maintain a much greater than usual gap from the vehicle in front. Accelerate, steer and brake as delicately as possible in the highest appropriate gear and drive more slowly than usual. Remember to wash salt and grit from your vehicle, especially its underside, as soon as you can, to reduce risk of corrosion.

Q 189 You are driving in freezing conditions. What should you do when approaching a sharp left-hand bend?

Mark two answers
- **A.** Slow down before you reach the bend
- **B.** Gently apply your handbrake
- **C.** Firmly use your footbrake
- **D.** Coast into the bend
- **E.** Avoid sudden steering movements

The safest way to brake is progressively when your vehicle is in gear and travelling in a straight line. Progressive braking is absolutely essential in icy conditions.

Q 190 How should you drive around a bend on ice?

Mark one answer

- **A.** Using the clutch and brake together
- **B.** In first gear
- **C.** Braking as you enter the bend
- **D.** Slowly and smoothly

You cause skidding by changing your vehicle's speed and/or direction more harshly than your tyre grip can handle. Sudden braking, sudden cornering or both may make your tyres lose grip. On a slippery road surface your vehicle may skid. Try to avoid skidding by accelerating gently, steering smoothly and braking progressively. See **Q192** and **Q319**.

Q 191 Skidding is mainly caused by

Mark one answer

- **A.** The weather
- **B.** The driver
- **C.** The vehicle
- **D.** The road

Skidding occurs when the tyres lose their grip on the road usually as a result of accelerating, braking or changing direction too harshly or suddenly for the surface conditions.

Q 192 To correct a rear-wheel skid you should

Mark one answer

- **A.** Not turn at all
- **B.** Turn away from it
- **C.** Turn into it
- **D.** Apply your handbrake

In any skid, you should keep a light grip on the steering wheel with both hands. Your first reaction should be immediately to release your brake pedal completely. For a rear-wheel skid, steer left if the rear of the car is sliding to the left. Steer right if the rear of the car is sliding to the right. Never oversteer and cause a skid in the opposite direction. For a front-wheel skid, release your accelerator pedal immediately. Wait for your front tyres to regain some grip before you try to steer. Remember that it is better to avoid a skid in the first place. Skidding on the public highway is not only dangerous but illegal. See **Q190** and **Q319**.

Q 193 Why should you test your brakes after this hazard?

Mark one answer

- **A.** Because you will be driving on a slippery road
- **B.** Because your brakes will be soaking wet
- **C.** Because you will have driven down a long hill
- **D.** Because you will have just crossed a long bridge

When you press your brake pedal you force together surfaces of the drum and/or disc brakes. Friction between the drum linings or between the pads and discs slows your wheels down. Your braking efficiency is reduced if the friction surfaces wear out or become coated in dirt, oil or water. Friction makes the brakes hot and helps to keep them dry.

Q 194 You are driving along a country road. You see this sign. AFTER dealing safely with the hazard you should always

Ford

Mark one answer

- [ ] **A.** Check your tyre pressures
- [ ] **B.** Switch on your hazard warning lights
- [ ] **C.** Switch on your rear fog lamps
- [ ] **D.** Test your brakes

See **Q193**, **Q322** and **Q555**.

Q 195 You keep well back while waiting to overtake a large vehicle. Another car fills the gap. You should

Mark one answer

- [ ] **A.** Sound your horn
- [ ] **B.** Drop back further
- [ ] **C.** Flash your headlights
- [ ] **D.** Start to overtake

Remember that only you can ensure a suitable gap from the vehicle immediately in front of yours. Keep a sufficient space and keep safe.

Q 196 You are following a vehicle at a safe distance on a wet road. Another driver overtakes you and pulls into the gap you have left. What should you do?

Mark one answer

- [ ] **A.** Flash your headlights as a warning
- [ ] **B.** Try to overtake safely as soon as you can
- [ ] **C.** Drop back to regain a safe distance
- [ ] **D.** Stay close to the other vehicle until it moves on

On a wet road keep at least a four-second gap from the vehicle in front. The closer you are the more danger you are in and the more spray your wipers have to deal with. Remember that overtaking is the most dangerous manoeuvre, even in good conditions.

Q 197 You are driving at night. Why should you be extra careful of your speed?

Mark one answer

- [ ] **A.** Because you might need to stop within the distance that you can see
- [ ] **B.** Because it uses more petrol
- [ ] **C.** Because driving with the lights on runs down the battery
- [ ] **D.** Because you may be late

Remember the golden rule of The Highway Code: **drive at a speed that allows you to stop well within the distance you can see to be clear**. See **Q203**.

Q 198 You are on a narrow road at night. A slower-moving vehicle ahead has been signalling right for some time. What should you do?

Mark one answer

- [ ] **A.** Overtake on the left
- [ ] **B.** Flash your headlights before overtaking
- [ ] **C.** Signal right and sound your horn
- [ ] **D.** Wait for the signal to be cancelled before overtaking

Be patient, especially on narrow roads at night travelling behind a slow-moving vehicle. Take care always to cancel your signals after any manoeuvre so that you do not confuse other traffic.

Q 199 Which TWO of the following are correct? When overtaking at night you should

Mark two answers

- [ ] **A.** Wait until a bend so that you can see the oncoming headlights
- [ ] **B.** Sound your horn twice before moving out
- [ ] **C.** Be careful because you can see less
- [ ] **D.** Beware of bends in the road ahead
- [ ] **E.** Put headlights on full beam

Overtaking at night is even more dangerous than overtaking in daylight. Keep your headlights dipped but remember that even these could dazzle oncoming road users. Sounding your horn is an offence between 11.30pm and 7am in a built-up area. See **Q269**, **Q270** and **Q595**.

Q 200 You are driving at night with full beam headlights on. A vehicle is overtaking you. You should dip your lights

Mark one answer

- [ ] **A.** Some time after the vehicle has passed you
- [ ] **B.** Before the vehicle starts to pass you
- [ ] **C.** Only if the other driver dips his headlights
- [ ] **D.** As soon as the vehicle passes you

If you want to overtake at night and the vehicle you are following dips its headlights before you begin your manoeuvre, do not take this as a signal from the driver that it is safe to pass.

Q 201 You are overtaking a car at night. You must be sure that

Mark one answer

- [ ] **A.** You flash your headlamps before overtaking
- [ ] **B.** Your rear fog lights are switched on
- [ ] **C.** You have switched your lights to full beam before overtaking
- [ ] **D.** You do not dazzle other road users

It is extremely dangerous and an offence to dazzle other road users with your headlights. Be prepared to dip your headlights well before you enter a bend. This is especially important on a left-hand bend where your headlight beam is bound to shine into the faces of oncoming drivers.

Q 202 You are travelling at night. You are dazzled by headlights coming towards you. You should

Mark one answer
- **A.** Pull down your sun visor
- **B.** Slow down or stop
- **C.** Switch on your main beam headlights
- **D.** Put your hand over your eyes

You can reduce the risk of being dazzled by oncoming headlights if you focus your eyes on the road ahead and towards the left-hand verge. Never look directly into oncoming headlights. Do not use your sun visor, tinted glasses or lenses. Keep your windows clean inside and out. Do not apply spray-on or other tinting materials to them.

Q 203 You are dazzled by oncoming headlights when driving at night. What should you do?

Mark one answer
- **A.** Slow down or stop
- **B.** Brake hard
- **C.** Drive faster past the oncoming car
- **D.** Flash your lights

When driving at night you must be able to stop within the distance of your headlight beam. This generally means you must drive more slowly after dark than in daylight. If you are dazzled by lights from another vehicle, you must at least slow down. Sometimes you need to pull over and stop. Although you can focus your attention on what you can see in the beam of your headlights, remember that some hazards up ahead may not be lit or easily seen.

Q 204 You are driving on a well-lit motorway at night. You must

Mark one answer
- **A.** Use only your sidelights
- **B.** Always use your headlights
- **C.** Always use rear fog lights
- **D.** Use headlights only in bad weather

At night your headlights will show up the reflective studs which mark the lanes and edges of the motorway. Your headlights will also show up more clearly the countdown markers to exits and other road signs.

Q 205 You are travelling on a motorway at night with other vehicles just ahead of you. Which lights should you have on?

Mark one answer
- **A.** Front fog lights
- **B.** Main beam headlights
- **C.** Sidelights only
- **D.** Dipped headlights

Use your headlights at night on motorways, even if they are well lit, and on roads with a speed limit greater than 50mph. Always dip your headlights when there is a risk of dazzling other road users you may be following.

Q 206 You are driving on a motorway at night. You MUST have your headlights switched on unless

Mark one answer

- **A.** There are vehicles close in front of you
- **B.** You are travelling below 50mph
- **C.** The motorway is lit
- **D.** Your vehicle is broken down on the hard shoulder

If you break down on the motorway, you should pull on to the hard shoulder, stop as far left as possible and switch on your hazard warning lights. At night or in poor visibility, switch off your headlights but keep your sidelights on.

Q 207 You are driving on a motorway in fog. The left-hand edge of the motorway can be identified by reflective studs. What colour are they?

Mark one answer

- **A.** Green
- **B.** Amber
- **C.** Red
- **D.** White

See **Q460** ,**Q461** and **Q465**.

Q 208 You should only use rear fog lights when you cannot see further than about

Mark one answer

- **A.** 100 metres (330 feet)
- **B.** 200 metres (660 feet)
- **C.** 250 metres (800 feet)
- **D.** 150 metres (495 feet)

Q 209 You should switch your rear fog lights on when visibility drops below

Mark one answer

- **A.** Your overall stopping distance
- **B.** 10 car lengths
- **C.** 10 metres (33 feet)
- **D.** 100 metres (330 feet)

Remember to switch off front and rear fog lights as soon as visibility improves, to avoid dazzling other road users. Always keep your windscreen and windows clean inside and out.

Q 210 You are driving in poor visibility. You can see more than 100 metres (330 feet) ahead. How can you make sure that other drivers can see you?

Mark one answer

- **A.** Turn on your dipped headlights
- **B.** Follow the vehicle in front closely
- **C.** Turn on your rear fog lights
- **D.** Keep well out towards the middle of the road

It is dangerous to use undipped headlights in fog. You may dazzle yourself as well as other road users because on main beam the headlights will reflect back off the fog.

Q 211 You are following other vehicles in fog with your lights on. How else can you reduce the chances of being involved in an accident?

Mark one answer

- **A.** Keep close to the vehicle in front
- **B.** Use your main beam instead of dipped headlights
- **C.** Keep together with the faster vehicles
- **D.** Reduce your speed and increase the gap

In fog you may not be able to see what faces the vehicle in front of yours. If you drive too close and too fast you may become part of a pile-up if the vehicles in front stop suddenly. Keep your headlights dipped. On main beam they can dazzle the driver in front and reflect back off the fog to dazzle you as well.

Q 212 Whilst driving, the fog clears and you can see more clearly. You must remember to

Mark one answer

- **A.** Switch off the fog lights
- **B.** Reduce your speed
- **C.** Switch off the demister
- **D.** Close any open windows

You may use fog lights if visibility is seriously reduced. It is an offence to use them at other times.

Q 213 You have to make a journey in foggy conditions. You should

Mark one answer

- **A.** Follow closely other vehicles' tail lights
- **B.** Never use demisters and windscreen wipers
- **C.** Leave plenty of time for your journey
- **D.** Keep two seconds behind other vehicles

If you must drive in fog, you must be prepared to drive more slowly than usual and to keep a greater distance from the vehicle in front than you should in perfect conditions.

Q 214 You have to make a journey in fog. What are the TWO most important things you should do before you set out?

Mark two answers

- **A.** Top up the radiator with antifreeze
- **B.** Make sure that you have a warning triangle in the vehicle
- **C.** Check that your lights are working
- **D.** Check the battery
- **E.** Make sure that the windows are clean

Remember it is an offence to drive a vehicle with defective lights even in daytime when they are not needed. In fog you need your dipped headlights to see and be seen. You also need to clean your windscreen and windows thoroughly to help prevent them from misting up.

Q 215 You are driving in fog. The car behind seems to be very close. You should

Mark one answer

- [ ] **A.** Switch on your hazard warning lights
- [ ] **B.** Pull over and stop immediately
- [ ] **C.** Speed up to get away
- [ ] **D.** Continue cautiously

Do not hang on the tail of the vehicle in front, especially in thick fog, unless you are travelling very slowly. If a vehicle hangs on your tail, all you can do is proceed slowly with care.

Q 216 Why should you always reduce your speed when driving in fog?

Mark one answer

- [ ] **A.** Because the brakes do not work as well
- [ ] **B.** Because you could be dazzled by other people's fog lights
- [ ] **C.** Because the engine's colder
- [ ] **D.** Because it is more difficult to see events ahead

When you drive in fog you cannot see clearly very far ahead. The sudden appearance of a hazard may force you to stop without being able to give much warning to traffic behind you. Even at low speeds this can lead to damaging rear-end shunts.

Q 217 You are driving in fog. Why should you keep well back from the vehicle in front?

Mark one answer

- [ ] **A.** In case it changes direction suddenly
- [ ] **B.** In case its fog lights dazzle you
- [ ] **C.** In case it stops suddenly
- [ ] **D.** In case its brake lights dazzle you

Remember your Highway Code: **drive at a speed that allows you to stop well within the distance you can see to be clear.**

Q 218 You have to park on the road in fog. You should

Mark one answer

- [ ] **A.** Leave sidelights on
- [ ] **B.** Leave dipped headlights and fog lights on
- [ ] **C.** Leave dipped headlights on
- [ ] **D.** Leave main beam headlights on

It is an offence to leave headlamps on when stopped or to park without side, tail or registration plate lamps on unless unlit parking is allowed. It is extremely dangerous to park on the road in fog. If you must park in fog, you should leave your sidelights on, even if you could park without lights normally.

Q 219 On a foggy day you unavoidably have to park your car on the road. You should

Mark one answer

- [ ] **A.** Leave your headlights on
- [ ] **B.** Leave your fog lights on
- [ ] **C.** Leave your sidelights on
- [ ] **D.** Leave your hazard lights on

Q 220 Which THREE are suitable restraints for a child under three years?

Mark three answers

- [ ] **A.** A child seat
- [ ] **B.** An adult holding a child
- [ ] **C.** An adult seat belt
- [ ] **D.** A lap belt
- [ ] **E.** A harness
- [ ] **F.** A baby carrier

The seat belt law requires the driver and passengers of all ages in the front of the vehicle to be restrained unless exempt on medical or other grounds. Passengers travelling in the rear of cars or taxis must be restrained where a seat belt is fitted and available. Ideally, a child under 3 years of age should be protected by a purpose-designed restraint appropriate to the child's weight. A carry cot held by straps or an infant carrier is suitable for a child under 1 year old. For a child over 1 but under 3 years of age an appropriate child seat or booster cushion with an adult belt is suitable. If a seat belt is not available in the rear, a child under 3 years old should be restrained by an adult.

Q 221 Would it be safe to allow children to sit BEHIND the rear seats of a hatchback car?

Mark one answer
- **A.** Yes, if you can see clearly to the rear
- **B.** Yes, if they're under 11 years
- **C.** No, unless all the other seats are full
- **D.** No, not in any circumstances

Never carry children behind the rear seats of an estate car or hatchback. If you stopped suddenly in an emergency, they would be thrown forward with considerable force against the windscreen, the other passengers or yourself. This could result in severe injuries or even death.

Q 222 What do child locks in a vehicle do?

Mark one answer
- **A.** Lock the seat belt buckles in place
- **B.** Lock the rear windows in the up position
- **C.** Stop children from opening rear doors
- **D.** Stop the rear seats from tipping forward

Children can do what you least expect. They have been known to undo their restraint and open a door whilst the car is travelling at speed. Make sure you set the child locks of the rear doors when you have children in the back. If possible have an adult passenger with you to keep an eye on them.

Q 223 Your car is fitted with child safety door locks. When used this means that normally

Mark one answer
- **A.** The rear doors can only be opened from the outside
- **B.** The rear doors can only be opened from the inside
- **C.** All the doors can only be opened from the outside
- **D.** All the doors can only be opened from the inside

Child-proof safety locks can only be put on or taken off when the rear doors are opened to allow access to a small lever built into the doors themselves.

Q 224 Your vehicle is fitted with child safety door locks. You should use these so that children inside the car cannot open

Mark one answer
- **A.** The right-hand doors
- **B.** The left-hand doors
- **C.** The rear doors
- **D.** Any of the doors

Child-proof safety locks are independent of any central locking system. Adult passengers travelling in the rear of your car may be irritated if they cannot open their door.

Q 225 When your vehicle is loaded you MUST make sure that the load will

Mark one answer

- **A.** Remain secure
- **B.** Be easy to unload
- **C.** Not be damaged
- **D.** Not damage the vehicle

> As the driver, you are responsible for the vehicle you are driving even if you are still a new learner. You would be the one committing an offence if your vehicle is in any way unroadworthy, for example by being overloaded or having an insecure load. See **Q226** and **Q351**.

Q 226 Any load that is carried on a roof rack MUST be

Mark one answer

- **A.** Securely fastened when driving
- **B.** Carried only when strictly necessary
- **C.** As light as possible
- **D.** Covered with plastic sheeting

> Causing danger by carrying an insecure load is an offence. Luggage on a roof rack increases fuel consumption and running costs. Overloading the roof rack makes a car less stable and could provide an insurance company with a reason for not honouring a claim. If something (say a ladder) on the roof rack overhangs your vehicle by more than 2m (6½ feet) you must make the overhang obvious to other road users. You could fix a projection triangle or tie a red cloth to the overhanging end of the load. See **Q225** and **Q351**.

Q 227 You should load a trailer so that the weight is

Mark one answer

- **A.** Mostly over the nearside wheel
- **B.** Evenly distributed
- **C.** Mainly at the front
- **D.** Mostly at the rear

> It is an offence to tow a trailer which is overloaded or which has an insecure or dangerously projecting load. When you are towing a trailer (or caravan) the national speed limit is 50mph on single-carriageway roads and 60mph on dual carriageways and motorways. And you must not park on the road at night without lights.

Q 228 Before towing a caravan you should ensure that heavy items in it are loaded

Mark one answer

- **A.** As high as possible, mainly over the axle(s)
- **B.** As low as possible, mainly over the axle(s)
- **C.** As low as possible, forward of the axle(s)
- **D.** As high as possible, forward of the axle(s)

> Racing cars are built to be as low to the ground as possible to minimise their tendency to tip over, especially when cornering. If you are towing a trailer or caravan, make sure its gross laden weight does not exceed 85% of the kerbside weight of your car and its nose weight does not exceed the maximum downward load of your car's towing hitch.

Q 229 Are passengers allowed to ride in a caravan that is being towed?

Mark one answer

- **A.** Yes
- **B.** No
- **C.** Only if all the seats in the towing vehicle are full
- **D.** Only if a stabiliser is fitted

Just as no one should travel in a towed caravan, no one should travel in the boot of a hatchback car. See **Q221**.

Q 230 You are towing a small trailer on a busy three-lane motorway. All the lanes are open. You must

Mark two answers

- **A.** Not exceed 60mph
- **B.** Not overtake
- **C.** Have a stabiliser fitted
- **D.** Use only the left and centre lanes

Different motorway restrictions apply to different vehicles. The speed limits are 70mph and 60mph unless signs indicate otherwise. You would need to travel a very long distance at 60mph to overtake a long vehicle travelling at 59mph.

Q 231 If a trailer swerves or snakes when you are towing it you should

Mark one answer

- **A.** Ease off the accelerator and reduce your speed
- **B.** Let go of the steering wheel and let it correct itself
- **C.** Brake hard and hold the pedal down
- **D.** Increase your speed as quickly as possible

Experienced drivers know how to adjust their speed to the changing road conditions so that their caravan or trailer remains stable.

Q 232 You are towing a caravan. Which is the safest type of rear-view mirror to use?

Mark one answer

- **A.** Interior wide-angle-view mirror
- **B.** Extended-arm side mirrors
- **C.** Ordinary door mirrors
- **D.** Ordinary interior mirror

Towing a caravan is similar to driving a large articulated lorry and having to rely on external mirrors to check on the traffic conditions behind the caravan or lorry.

Q 233 How can you stop a caravan snaking from side to side?

Mark one answer

- **A.** Turn the steering wheel slowly to each side
- **B.** Accelerate to increase your speed
- **C.** Stop as quickly as you can
- **D.** Slow down very gradually

The higher the speed the greater the risk of a caravan or trailer snaking. The maximum speed you are allowed to drive at when towing a caravan or trailer is 60mph on dual carriageways or motorways. Remember that towing becomes more dangerous in windy conditions.

Q 234 You are towing a trailer and experience snaking. How would you reduce it?

Mark one answer

- **A.** Ease off the accelerator slowly
- **B.** Press the accelerator firmly
- **C.** Steer sharply
- **D.** Brake hard

If you are steering in a straight line and you feel your car and caravan starting to swing from side to side, this is a sure sign that you are travelling too fast. If you apply your brakes too soon and too hard there is a risk of the caravan jack-knifing.

Q 235 Your vehicle pulls to one side when braking. You should

Mark one answer

- **A.** Change the tyres around
- **B.** Consult your garage as soon as possible
- **C.** Pump the pedal when braking
- **D.** Use your handbrake at the same time

Brake pull could be caused by faulty brakes, suspension or steering. Your garage may need to readjust the brakes, tighten a component or replace friction material contaminated by grease, oil or brake fluid. If your vehicle pulls to one side when you are not braking, you should check the wear and pressure of your tyres and test for worn shock absorbers. See **Q236**.

Q 236 You are testing your suspension. You notice that your vehicle keeps bouncing when you press down on the front wing. What does this mean?

Mark one answer

- **A.** Worn tyres
- **B.** Tyres under-inflated
- **C.** Steering wheel not located centrally
- **D.** Worn shock absorbers

Good defensive drivers become used to the way their car handles and sounds. They can usually feel and hear the warning signs of a fault developing. When you detect a fault, take steps to prevent any serious damage or mechanical breakdown. As part of the MOT test the category Steering and Suspension includes steering control, wheel alignment, shock absorbers, wheel bearings, and front and rear suspension.

Q 237 It is important that tyre pressures are correct. They should be checked at least

Mark one answer

- **A.** Once a week
- **B.** Every time the vehicle is serviced
- **C.** Every four weeks
- **D.** Every time the vehicle has an MOT test

We should look at our tyres each day before we drive to check for obvious signs of damage. If a tyre pressure falls suddenly and significantly, it should be measured more than once a week. Faulty tyres should be repaired or replaced immediately.

Q 238 It is essential that tyre pressures are checked regularly. When should this be done?

Mark one answer

- **A.** After any lengthy journey
- **B.** After driving at high speed
- **C.** When tyres are hot
- **D.** When tyres are cold

The pressure recommended for a cold tyre allows for the increase in pressure when the tyre and the air inside it warm up on a journey. Check your tyres daily for signs of damage or excessive wear. A tyre needs repair if you have to inflate it every day.

Q 239 Why should tyres be kept to the pressure the manufacturer tells you?

Mark one answer
- **A.** To keep the car the right height off the road
- **B.** To save wear on the engine
- **C.** To stop the car from sloping to one side
- **D.** To help prevent the car from skidding

Tyres are your vehicle's contact with the road. If the pressure is too low, the tyre wall rapidly weakens and causes the tyre to fail. Higher tyre pressures are generally recommended for a heavily loaded car or for long journeys at high speeds. But you should avoid too high a pressure as it dangerously reduces the area of contact between the tyres and the road.

Q 240 The legal minimum depth of tread for car tyres over three-quarters of the breadth is

Mark one answer
- **A.** 2.5mm
- **B.** 4mm
- **C.** 1mm
- **D.** 1.6mm

This minimum tread depth must be continuous around the tyre and across the central three-quarters of its width. For vehicles other than cars, light vans and light trailers, the minimum tread depth is 1mm.

Q 241 What can cause heavy steering?

Mark one answer
- **A.** Driving on ice
- **B.** Badly worn brakes
- **C.** Over-inflated tyres
- **D.** Under-inflated tyres

It is an offence to drive a vehicle with low tyre pressures. Your car becomes difficult to control and your overall stopping distances increase. You could lose up to 13% tread mileage if your tyre pressure is only 90% of the manufacturer's recommended value.

Q 242 Driving with under-inflated tyres can affect

Mark two answers
- **A.** Engine temperature
- **B.** Fuel consumption
- **C.** Braking
- **D.** Oil pressure

It takes very little time to check tyre pressures but the time spent could save money and lives.

Q 243 Excessive or uneven tyre wear can be caused by faults in the

Mark two answers
- **A.** Braking system
- **B.** Suspension
- **C.** Gearbox
- **D.** Exhaust system

Harsh acceleration and braking, sharp cornering at high speeds and other forms of bad driving on the public highway can cause excessive and uneven tyre wear.

Q 244 It is illegal to drive with tyres that

Mark one answer

- [ ] **A.** Have a large deep cut in the side wall
- [ ] **B.** Have been bought second-hand
- [ ] **C.** Are of different makes
- [ ] **D.** Have painted walls

Ideally all the tyres fitted to your vehicle should be of the same make and have the same pattern with the same amount of tread. Radial tyres have walls flexible enough to allow an even road contact especially when cornering. Some radials have steel bracing. Others have textile bracing. The two types must never be mixed on the same axle. If used in combination, steel radials must be fitted to the rear wheels and the textile radials fitted to the front wheels. The earlier crossply tyre is incompatible with the more common radial tyre. Do not mix them and never on the same axle.

Q 245 Which THREE does the law require you to keep in good condition?

Mark three answers

- [ ] **A.** Gears
- [ ] **B.** Clutch
- [ ] **C.** Headlights
- [ ] **D.** Windscreen
- [ ] **E.** Seat belts

If your car is more than 3 years old, your lights, windscreen and seat belts and their anchorage will be examined as part of its MOT test. You must keep your windscreen clean and clear. It is an offence to drive with defective lights even in daylight or with a dirty or obscured windscreen.

Q 246 Which FOUR of these must be in good working order for your car to be roadworthy?

Mark four answers

- [ ] **A.** Temperature gauge
- [ ] **B.** Speedometer
- [ ] **C.** Windscreen washers
- [ ] **D.** Windscreen wipers
- [ ] **E.** Oil warning light
- [ ] **F.** Horn

You should test your horn and washers daily. It is an offence to drive with defective windscreen washers or with an empty washer bottle. Not only must your speedometer work, it must also be accurate to within 10%. Never use its possible inaccuracy as an excuse to break speed limits. See **Q269**, **Q270** and **Q595**.

Q 247 Give two reasons for using an additive in the windscreen washer reservoir.

Mark two answers

- [ ] **A.** To prevent freezing in winter
- [ ] **B.** To wipe off leaves in autumn
- [ ] **C.** To help prevent mould growth
- [ ] **D.** To clear dead insects in summer
- [ ] **E.** To prevent corrosion

The water in the washer bottle should contain a small amount of detergent to help keep the windscreen clean and free of streaks. In winter it should also contain a small amount of an antifreeze to keep the windscreen clear and free of ice.

Q 248 Which of these, if allowed to get low, could cause an accident?

Mark one answer

- [ ] **A.** Antifreeze level
- [ ] **B.** Brake fluid level
- [ ] **C.** Battery water level
- [ ] **D.** Radiator coolant level

You should keep your radiator topped up with appropriate coolant and be sure to include antifreeze for the winter months. If your battery is not a sealed unit you should keep it topped up with distilled water.

Q 249 The main cause of brake fade is

Mark one answer

- [ ] **A.** The brakes overheating
- [ ] **B.** Air in the brake fluid
- [ ] **C.** Oil on the brakes
- [ ] **D.** The brakes out of adjustment

It is wise to check your brake fluid level weekly or when you refuel and check the engine oil level. If the fluid is leaking and you have to pump your pedal or push it an unusually long way down before your brakes work, take the car to your garage. Take notice of other symptoms of brake faults such as grab, fade, judder and squeal. It is very dangerous and an offence to drive a vehicle with defective brakes.

Q 250 When are you allowed to drive if your brake lights DO NOT work?

Mark one answer

- [ ] **A.** During the daytime
- [ ] **B.** When going for an MOT test
- [ ] **C.** At no time
- [ ] **D.** In an emergency

You signal to traffic behind you every time you press the brake pedal. So use your mirror before you do. Remember MSM (Mirror–Signal–Manoeuvre) whenever you intend to change speed and/or direction. See **Q580.**

Q 251 New petrol-engined cars must be fitted with catalytic converters. The reason for this is to

Mark one answer

- [ ] **A.** Control exhaust noise levels
- [ ] **B.** Prolong the life of the exhaust system
- [ ] **C.** Allow the exhaust system to be recycled
- [ ] **D.** Reduce harmful exhaust emissions

The noise of an exhaust is controlled by the design of the system, expansion chamber and silencer box, all of which will be corroded by the hot, moist exhaust fumes. Catalytic converters lower the amount of carbon monoxide in the fumes by helping it to burn into carbon dioxide.

Q 252 If you notice a strong smell of petrol as you drive along you should

Mark one answer

- [ ] **A.** Not worry, as it is only exhaust fumes
- [ ] **B.** Carry on at a reduced speed
- [ ] **C.** Expect it to stop in a few miles
- [ ] **D.** Stop and investigate the problem

Bear in mind that there is always a risk of fire with petrol and its vapour. When you refuel take care never to overfill the tank. Always replace the petrol cap firmly. Remember it is an offence to drive a vehicle emitting excessive fumes.

Q 253 In which of these containers may you carry petrol in a motor vehicle?

A

B

C

D

Mark one answer

☐ **A.** A
☐ **B.** B
☐ **C.** C
☐ **D.** D

Try to plan any journey so that you do not need to carry extra fuel. The greater your car load the more fuel your engine will use. The fuel in your tank is part of your car's load. If you are only making short journeys it is more economical **not** to keep your tank full up.

Q 254 Why is it important that footwear is suitable for driving?

Mark one answer

☐ **A.** To help you adjust your seat
☐ **B.** To enable you to walk for assistance should you need to
☐ **C.** To maintain control of the pedals
☐ **D.** To prevent wear on the pedals

Q 255 It is important to wear suitable shoes when you're driving. Why is this?

Mark one answer

☐ **A.** To prevent wear on the pedals
☐ **B.** To maintain control of the pedals
☐ **C.** To enable you to adjust your seat
☐ **D.** To enable you to walk for assistance if you break down

The law allows you to drive in bare feet but it is not recommended. Try to keep for driving a pair of comfortable, flat-heeled shoes with non-slip soles of medium thickness. Very thin soles can be tiring. Very thick soles can make it difficult to 'feel' the pedals.

Q 256 What is the most important factor in avoiding running into the car in front?

Mark one answer

☐ **A.** Making sure your brakes are efficient
☐ **B.** Always driving at a steady speed
☐ **C.** Keeping the correct separation distance
☐ **D.** Having tyres that meet the legal requirements

Good drivers adjust their speed to maintain a safe distance from the vehicle in front. If your brakes develop a fault when you are out driving you will certainly need to increase the gap between you and the vehicle in front. Remember it is dangerous and against the law to drive with defective brakes and faulty tyres.

Q 257 What will cause high fuel consumption?

Mark one answer

- [ ] **A.** Poor steering control
- [ ] **B.** Accelerating around bends
- [ ] **C.** Driving in high gears
- [ ] **D.** Harsh braking and accelerating

You could save at least 15% on your fuel bill by planning your driving. Good drivers avoid harsh acceleration and braking. For more economical and environmentally friendly motoring you should drive at appropriate, modest speeds in the highest suitable gear.

Q 258 You cannot see clearly behind when reversing. What should you do?

Mark one answer

- [ ] **A.** Open your window to look behind
- [ ] **B.** Open the door and look behind
- [ ] **C.** Look in the nearside mirror
- [ ] **D.** Ask someone to guide you

Because part of the road you are reversing along will be hidden in your blind spots, there is always the risk of running over pedestrians – particularly children. Always reverse with great care and, wherever possible, get someone to guide you back.

Q 259 A car driver MUST ensure that seat belts are worn by

Mark one answer

- [ ] **A.** All front-seat passengers
- [ ] **B.** All passengers
- [ ] **C.** All rear-seat passengers
- [ ] **D.** Children under 14

The seat belt law requires the driver and passengers of all ages in the front of the vehicle to be restrained unless exempt on medical or other grounds. Passengers travelling in the rear of cars or taxis must be restrained where a seat belt is fitted and available. The driver is responsible for himself and for any children under 14 years of age.

Q 260 You are carrying two children and their parents in your car. Who is responsible for seeing that the children wear seat belts?

Mark one answer

- [ ] **A.** The children's parents
- [ ] **B.** You
- [ ] **C.** The front-seat passenger
- [ ] **D.** The children

Anyone driving a car, even a learner under supervision, is responsible for ensuring that any children under the age of 14 are wearing seat belts if fitted. When there are insufficient belts for the rear seat passengers, it is safer for adults to be restrained. For children aged 1 to 4 years old, it is safer to wear an adult belt alone rather than no restraint at all.

Q 261 Car passengers MUST wear a seat belt if one is available, unless they are

Mark one answer

- [ ] **A.** Under 14 years old
- [ ] **B.** Under 1.5 metres (5 feet) in height
- [ ] **C.** Sitting in the rear seat
- [ ] **D.** Exempt for medical reasons

Seat belts must be available for the driver and front seat passengers. All cars built after 1981 have anchorage points for rear seat belts. More recent cars have rear seat belts fitted.

Q 262 What will reduce the risk of neck injury resulting from a collision?

Mark one answer

- **A.** An air-sprung seat
- **B.** Anti-lock brakes
- **C.** A collapsible steering wheel
- **D.** A properly adjusted head restraint

Anti-lock braking systems (ABS) are designed to allow you to brake in an emergency while at the same time maintaining control of the steering.

Q 263 A properly adjusted head restraint will

Mark one answer

- **A.** Make you more comfortable
- **B.** Help you to avoid neck injury
- **C.** Help you to relax
- **D.** Help you to maintain your driving position

A whiplash injury to the neck usually happens when a stationary car is struck from behind by another vehicle. Bones in the neck can be damaged or fractured. Discs between the bones can be displaced. Nerves in the spinal column can be injured. A suitable headrest can prevent the head from being jerked backwards.

Q 264 While driving a warning light on your vehicle's instrument panel comes on. You should

Mark one answer

- **A.** Continue if the engine sounds all right
- **B.** Hope that it is just a temporary electrical fault
- **C.** Deal with the problem when there is more time
- **D.** Check out the problem quickly and safely

Good drivers will understand the international standard symbols on their vehicle's panel lights and know what to do if any of the lights give a warning. A red light means danger and amber means caution. Green tells you something is working (e.g. direction indicators) and blue shows that your headlights are on full beam.

Q 265 When may you use hazard warning lights?

Mark one answer

- **A.** To park alongside another car
- **B.** To park on double yellow lines
- **C.** When you are being towed
- **D.** When you have broken down

Hazard warning lights are for use in an emergency. They are your four indicator lights all flashing in unison. The flashing amber lights warn other road users of your presence and of a likely obstruction to their progress. Switching on your hazard warning lights does not allow you to park illegally or to ignore parking restrictions.

Q 266 Hazard warning lights should be used when vehicles are

Mark one answer

- **A.** Broken down and causing an obstruction
- **B.** Faulty and moving slowly
- **C.** Being towed along a road
- **D.** Reversing into a side road

> You should use hazard warning lights only in an emergency. Normally you use them when you are not moving and causing a temporary obstruction because your vehicle has broken down. You may use them when moving only if you are on a motorway or unrestricted dual carriageway and you need to warn drivers behind you of a hazard or obstruction ahead. See **Q347–Q350** and **Q482**.

Q 267 When may you use hazard warning lights when driving?

Mark one answer

- **A.** Instead of sounding the horn in a built-up area between 11.30pm and 7am
- **B.** On a motorway or unrestricted dual carriageway, to warn of a hazard ahead
- **C.** On rural routes, after a warning sign of animals
- **D.** On the approach to toucan crossings, where cyclists are waiting to cross

> See **Q266**.

Q 268 You are driving on a clear night. There is a steady stream of oncoming traffic. The national speed limit applies. Which lights should you use?

Mark one answer

- **A.** Full beam headlights
- **B.** Sidelights
- **C.** Dipped headlights
- **D.** Fog lights

> Use dipped headlights in poor daytime visibility so that other road users can see you. Remember it is an offence not to use them and an offence to dazzle other road users with undipped headlights.

Q 269 You must NOT sound your horn

Mark one answer

- **A.** Between 10pm and 6am in a built-up area
- **B.** At any time in a built-up area
- **C.** Between 11.30pm and 7am in a built-up area
- **D.** Between 11.30pm and 6am on any road

> It is normally an offence to sound your horn if you car is not moving or if you are in a built-up area between 11.30pm and 7am.

Q 270 When should you NOT use your horn in a built-up area?

Mark one answer

- [ ] **A.** Between 8pm and 8am
- [ ] **B.** Between 9pm and dawn
- [ ] **C.** Between dusk and 8am
- [ ] **D.** Between 11.30pm and 7am

> You may sound your horn or flash your lights to warn others of your presence or when there is danger from another moving vehicle. After dark it may be more appropriate just to flash your lights. Never sound your horn as a greeting or to express your annoyance. See **Q38** and **Q595**.

Q 271 When you approach a bus signalling to move off from a bus stop you should

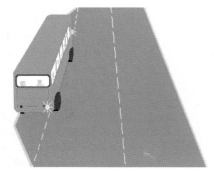

Mark one answer

- [ ] **A.** Get past before it moves
- [ ] **B.** Allow it to pull away, if it is safe to do so
- [ ] **C.** Flash your headlamps as you approach
- [ ] **D.** Signal left and wave the bus on

> Buses run to a timetable. The Highway Code tells you to give way to them 'whenever you can do so safely, especially when they signal to pull away from bus stops'. Remember to look out for passengers leaving the bus and stepping into the road.

The three topics in this section are about **other types of vehicle, safety margins** and **accidents**. The first concerns other vehicle characteristics. The second topic relates safety to weather and road conditions. The last is about accident risks and accident handling.

OTHER TYPES OF VEHICLE

Motorcycles, articulated lorries, buses, coaches and high-sided vans all differ in their manoeuvrability and in the size of the driver's field of vision. They need different times and distances to speed up, slow down and stop. Road and weather conditions can have different effects on different vehicles. Some vehicles can worsen the effects of road and weather conditions on other vehicles. A large lorry may throw spray on to following vehicles and suddenly alter the wind force on passing vehicles. Good drivers bear these factors in mind when assessing the risks of approaching hazards.

SAFETY MARGINS

Good drivers know the correct stopping distances and how changing conditions can affect safety margins. You need to know how to cope with snow, ice or fog. You also need to know what to do if you encounter flooding or a ford. We should drive more slowly after dark than we do in daylight so that we can stop safely within the distance visible in our headlights.

ACCIDENTS

Some road users are more at risk than others. Pedestrians are very vulnerable, especially if they are children, elderly, disabled or impaired. You should know that a pedestrian carrying a white stick with two red reflective bands is blind and deaf. You should allow for the possibility that a pedestrian may not see you, may misjudge your speed or may be unable to react quickly enough to your approach. If hit by a car travelling at 20mph, a pedestrian will be injured, not always seriously, or may be killed. If hit at 40mph, the pedestrian is usually killed. Any surviving pedestrian will usually have very serious injuries. Cyclists or horse riders, especially if they are children, are at risk on the road. You must know what to do if you meet them.

At a traffic accident there is always a risk of danger to yourself and others from *fire* and *further collisions*. Use your hazard warning lights and red triangle to warn other traffic. Make sure someone calls the emergency services, no one smokes and everyone switches off their engine. Do not move any casualties unless they are in danger. If a casualty has widely dilated pupils their heart may have stopped beating. Give priority to resuscitating anyone who has stopped breathing and to helping anyone who is bleeding heavily. Do **not** give casualties anything to drink.

By law you **must stop** if you are involved in an accident that causes damage or injury. You must give your name, address and vehicle registration number to anyone with reasonable grounds for requiring them. If you even slightly damage a parked vehicle and there is no one present at the scene, you must report the accident *in person* to the police as soon as possible and certainly within no more than 24 hours. If someone is injured, you must show your insurance certificate to the police at the time of the accident or take it to a police station within 24 hours. You should report the details of any accident to your insurance company even if you will not be making a claim against your insurance. Always follow the procedures recommended by your insurers when you record details of the accident and take names, addresses and statements from any witnesses.

Q 272 You are travelling behind a bus that pulls up at a bus stop. What should you do?

Mark two answers
- **A.** Accelerate past the bus sounding your horn
- **B.** Watch carefully for pedestrians
- **C.** Be ready to give way to the bus
- **D.** Pull in closely behind the bus

As part of their routine to assess the hazards ahead, good drivers will look to see how many people are waiting at a bus stop and how many passengers are going to get off a bus pulling up at the stop in front of them. See **Q271** and **Q595**.

Q 273 When following a large vehicle you should keep well back because

Mark one answer
- **A.** It allows the driver to see you in his mirrors
- **B.** It helps the large vehicle to stop more easily
- **C.** It allows you to corner more quickly
- **D.** It helps you keep out of the wind

When you are following a large vehicle and especially when you are intending to overtake it, make sure that your position and speed allow the driver to see both you and your signal.

Q 274 You are following a long vehicle approaching a crossroads. The driver signals right but moves close to the left-hand kerb. What should you do?

Mark one answer
- **A.** Warn the driver of the wrong signal
- **B.** Wait behind the long vehicle
- **C.** Report the driver to the police
- **D.** Overtake on the right-hand side

Q 275 You are following a long vehicle. It approaches a crossroads and signals left, but moves out to the right. You should

Mark one answer
- **A.** Get closer in order to pass it quickly
- **B.** Stay well back and give it room
- **C.** Assume the signal's wrong and it's really turning right
- **D.** Overtake as it starts to slow down

When turning left or right at junctions and when dealing with roundabouts, buses, coaches and articulated lorries are forced to take a different path from a car. These long vehicles may signal right but swing out to the left before turning. This may seem strange to a new driver.

Q 276 Which vehicle might have to use a different course to normal at roundabouts?

Mark one answer
- [ ] **A.** Sports car
- [ ] **B.** Van
- [ ] **C.** Estate car
- [ ] **D.** Long vehicle

Remember that long, large vehicles and articulated lorries are slower and far more difficult to manoeuvre than cars and motorcycles.

Q 277 You are approaching a mini-roundabout. The long vehicle in front is signalling left but positioned over to the right. You should

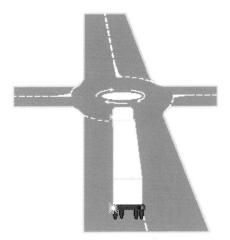

Mark one answer
- [ ] **A.** Sound your horn
- [ ] **B.** Overtake on the left
- [ ] **C.** Follow the same course as the lorry
- [ ] **D.** Keep well back

A large vehicle is forced to follow a course different from that of a car when turning at junctions and dealing with roundabouts. An articulated lorry may be signalling to go in one direction while swinging out towards the opposite direction. See **Q180, Q278, Q398** and **Q459**.

Q 278 You are following a large articulated vehicle. It is going to turn left into a narrow road. What action should you take?

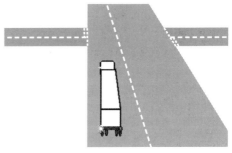

Mark one answer
- [ ] **A.** Move out and overtake on the offside
- [ ] **B.** Pass on the left as the vehicle moves out
- [ ] **C.** Be prepared to stop behind
- [ ] **D.** Overtake quickly before the lorry moves out

A large vehicle not only takes up far more of the road than a car does, it also takes more time to speed up and more time to slow down. You should appreciate the problems facing the drivers of large vehicles and make allowances when you encounter such vehicles. See **Q277**.

Q 279 Why is passing a lorry more risky than passing a car?

Mark one answer
- **A.** Lorries are longer than cars
- **B.** Lorries may suddenly pull up
- **C.** The brakes of lorries are not as good
- **D.** Lorries climb hills more slowly

> When you overtake a long lorry your car is likely to be further across on the wrong side of the road and for a longer time than it would be when you overtake another car. Two cars coming towards each other at 60mph will be closing the gap between them at 120mph and get 54m (176ft) closer together every second. If you need only 4 extra seconds to overtake a lorry, you would need to be at least an extra 50 car lengths away from the oncoming car.

Q 280 Before overtaking a large vehicle you should keep well back. Why is this?

Mark one answer
- **A.** To give acceleration space to overtake quickly on blind bends
- **B.** To get the best view of the road ahead
- **C.** To leave a gap in case the vehicle stops and rolls back
- **D.** To offer other drivers a safe gap if they want to overtake you

> It is difficult to see what traffic is in front of a large vehicle, especially if you are close behind. Good drivers stay well back to give themselves a clearer view of oncoming traffic. Bad drivers stay close up and then risk moving into the centre of the road to see oncoming traffic.

Q 281 The FIRST thing you should do when you want to overtake a large lorry is

Mark one answer
- **A.** Move close behind so that you can pass quickly
- **B.** Keep in close to the left-hand side
- **C.** Flash your headlights and wait for the driver to wave you on
- **D.** Stay well back to get a better view

> The normal driving routine of **M**irror–**S**ignal–**M**anoeuvre–**P**osition–**S**peed–**L**ook does **not** apply to overtaking. If you really must overtake another moving vehicle you need to get into the best position and speed to look for oncoming traffic: **PSL**. At the appropriate moment use your mirror to check again on the traffic behind you before you signal your intention to move out and overtake: **MSM**. See **Q283** and **Q515**.

Q 282 You wish to overtake a long, slow-moving vehicle on a busy road. You should

Mark one answer
- **A.** Wait behind until the driver waves you past
- **B.** Flash your headlights for the oncoming traffic to give way
- **C.** Follow it closely and keep moving out to see the road ahead
- **D.** Keep well back until you can see that it is clear

> You should not act on the signals of other drivers unauthorised to give them. Remember it is **your** responsiblity to ensure that it is safe to proceed. This applies even when you have been given the signal by a police officer or some other authorised person.

Q 283 When about to overtake a long vehicle you should

Mark one answer

- **A.** Sound the horn to warn the driver that you're there
- **B.** Stay well back from the lorry to obtain a better view
- **C.** Drive close to the lorry in order to pass more quickly
- **D.** Flash your lights and wait for the driver to signal when it is safe

> When you keep well back from any large vehicle, you only need to move very slightly to your right to get an even better view of oncoming traffic on the opposite side of road. Use your mirror before changing position. Signal when you intend to overtake. See **Q281** and **Q515**.

Q 284 You are following a large lorry on a wet road. Spray makes it difficult to see. You should

Mark one answer

- **A.** Drop back until you can see better
- **B.** Put your headlights on full beam
- **C.** Keep close to the lorry, away from the spray
- **D.** Speed up and overtake quickly

> Remember that your overall stopping distances on wet roads are at least double what they are on dry roads. Heavy spray from vehicles often acts like fog. It stops you from seeing oncoming traffic ahead on the other side of the road.

Q 285 You are driving on a wet motorway with surface spray. You should

Mark one answer

- **A.** Use your hazard flashers
- **B.** Use dipped headlights
- **C.** Use your rear fog lights
- **D.** Drive in any lane with no traffic

> When motorways are wet, the spray from traffic can produce foggy conditions. When this happens you should make sure that your vehicle can be seen by others. Do not use fog lights unless visibility is below 100m (330ft). Do not use hazard lights except in an emergency to warn others of danger up ahead.

Q 286 The road is wet. Why might a motorcyclist steer round drain covers on a bend?

Mark one answer

- **A.** To avoid puncturing the tyres on the edge of the drain covers
- **B.** To prevent the motorcycle sliding on the metal drain covers
- **C.** To help judge the bend using the drain covers as marker points
- **D.** To avoid splashing pedestrians on the pavement

> Road-holding depends upon friction between the tyres and the road surface. Water, oil and other liquids can drastically reduce tyre grip on a smooth surface, where friction is already low.

Q 287 Which of these vehicles is LEAST likely to be affected by crosswinds?

Mark one answer

- **A.** Cyclists
- **B.** Motorcyclists
- **C.** High-sided vehicles
- **D.** Cars

Two-wheeled vehicles are easily blown off course by strong crosswinds. You should give cyclists and motorcyclists extra room when overtaking them. High-sided vehicles and caravans can sometimes be blown over on to their side.

Q 288 In which THREE places could a strong crosswind affect your course?

Mark three answers

- **A.** After overtaking a large vehicle
- **B.** When passing gaps in hedges
- **C.** On exposed sections of roadway
- **D.** In towns
- **E.** In tunnels
- **F.** When passing parked vehicles

A strong wind is more dangerous when it blows in gusts, especially on exposed open roads. On a windy day you may experience the effect of gusting when you pass by large vehicles or gaps in hedges. In these conditions you need good control over your steering.

Q 289 It is very windy. You are about to overtake a motorcyclist. You should

Mark one answer

- **A.** Overtake slowly
- **B.** Allow extra room
- **C.** Sound your horn
- **D.** Keep close as you pass

Two-wheeled vehicles are easily blown off course by sudden gusts of wind created by passing cars and larger vehicles. To minimise this effect you should give cyclists and motorcyclists as much room as possible.

Q 290 It is very windy. You are behind a motorcyclist who is overtaking a high-sided vehicle. What should you do?

Mark one answer

- **A.** Overtake the motorcyclist immediately
- **B.** Keep well back
- **C.** Stay level with the motorcyclist
- **D.** Keep close to the motorcyclist

Motorcyclists may easily be blown off course by a strong gust as they overtake large vehicles shielding them from crosswinds. Even your car could briefly shield a two-wheeled vehicle from a crosswind. Always give motorcycles at least the same room that you would give another car.

Q 291 You're at a junction with limited visibility. You should

Mark one answer

- **A.** Inch forward, looking to the right
- **B.** Inch forward, looking to the left
- **C.** Inch forward, looking both ways
- **D.** Be ready to move off quickly

The majority of road accidents occur at junctions. The major cause is drivers looking but not really seeing and properly assessing the dangers. At junctions you should give priority to pedestrians on the road and to traffic on the major road. The usual order of priority given to traffic is:

1 turning left *into* a junction
2 turning left *out of* a junction
3 turning right *into* a junction
4 turning right *out of* a junction

Q 292 You are driving in a built-up area. You approach a speed hump. You should

Mark one answer

- **A.** Move across to the left-hand side of the road
- **B.** Wait for any pedestrians to cross
- **C.** Slow your vehicle right down
- **D.** Stop and check both pavements

Speed kills. Traffic calming systems and speed limits of 20mph or less are being introduced to reduce the risk of accidents to pedestrians. Always take extra care in the vicinity of young children, the elderly and the infirm. Drive very slowly over any speed hump, keeping your foot completely away from the accelerator pedal just as you do so. See **Q417**.

Q 293 You are approaching a bend at speed. You should begin to brake

Mark one answer

- **A.** On the bend
- **B.** After the bend
- **C.** After changing gears
- **D.** Before the bend

Use progressive braking when your car is travelling in a straight line to ensure that the tyre grip on the road surface is shared as evenly as possible by all the wheels.

Q 294 When approaching a right-hand bend you should keep well to the left. Why is this?

Mark one answer

- **A.** It improves your view of the road
- **B.** To overcome the effect of the road's slope
- **C.** It lets faster traffic from behind overtake
- **D.** To be positioned safely if the vehicle skids

Q 295 You are coming up to a right-hand bend. You should

Mark one answer

- **A.** Keep well to the left as it makes the bend faster
- **B.** Keep well to the left for a better view around the bend
- **C.** Keep well to the right to avoid anything in the gutter
- **D.** Keep well to the right to make the bend less sharp

Keep well away from any hazard lines along the centre of the road, especially on a bend. Never cross them to 'smooth out a corner'. They are there to separate the traffic. It is extremely dangerous and usually an offence to cross double white lines.

Q 296 You wish to park facing DOWNHILL. Which TWO of the following should you do?

Mark two answers

- [ ] **A.** Turn the steering wheel towards the kerb
- [ ] **B.** Park close to the bumper of another car
- [ ] **C.** Park with two wheels on the kerb
- [ ] **D.** Put the handbrake on firmly
- [ ] **E.** Turn the steering wheel away from the kerb

It is an offence to park on a pavement, even with just two wheels on the kerb. Your vehicle would be causing an obstruction. Park in forward gear facing uphill. If there is a kerb, turn your steering wheel away from it. If there is a soft verge or no kerb, turn your steering wheel towards the verge. Should your parking brakes fail, your car should be set to roll off the road, and not towards oncoming traffic.

Q 297 You are about to go down a steep hill. To control the speed of your vehicle you should

Mark one answer

- [ ] **A.** Select a high gear and use the brakes carefully
- [ ] **B.** Select a high gear and use the brakes firmly
- [ ] **C.** Select a low gear and use the brakes carefully
- [ ] **D.** Select a low gear and avoid using the brakes

Engine braking means keeping in gear and off the accelerator pedal. It does not mean selecting a lower gear and letting up the clutch pedal while the road speed of the vehicle is too high for the new gear.

Q 298 You are on a long, downhill slope. What should you do to help control the speed of your vehicle?

Mark one answer

- [ ] **A.** Grip the steering wheel tightly
- [ ] **B.** Select neutral
- [ ] **C.** Select a low gear
- [ ] **D.** Put the clutch down

Never coast downhill. Keep in gear so that you have engine braking as well as your footbrake. The lower the gear the stronger the engine braking. Remember that unnecessary coasting is dangerous and an offence.

Q 299 In very hot weather the road surface can get soft. Which TWO of the following will be affected most?

Mark two answers

- [ ] **A.** The suspension
- [ ] **B.** The steering
- [ ] **C.** Braking
- [ ] **D.** The windscreen

Your control over your car's speed and direction depends upon the grip of your tyres on the road. Any change of road surface affecting tyre grip will affect your steering and braking. A firm surface gives more grip than a soft surface. A dry surface gives more grip than a wet one.

Q 300 In windy conditions you need to take extra care when

Mark one answer

- [ ] **A.** Using the brakes
- [ ] **B.** Making a hill start
- [ ] **C.** Turning into a narrow road
- [ ] **D.** Passing pedal cyclists

Two-wheeled vehicles are more easily blown off course than other vehicles. Young children on bicycles are more vulnerable than adults on cycles or riders on mopeds or motorcycles.

Q 301 Where are you most likely to be affected by a crosswind?

Mark one answer

- **A.** On a narrow country lane
- **B.** On an open stretch of road
- **C.** On a busy stretch of road
- **D.** On a long, straight road

Traffic on a busy road and hedges along country lanes can give you some protection from crosswinds. On long, straight roads you can adjust your steering to allow for a crosswind. Driving along an open stretch of road on a windy day needs care, especially as the wind direction will change when the road changes direction.

Q 302 You are driving on the motorway in windy conditions. When passing high-sided vehicles you should

Mark one answer

- **A.** Increase your speed
- **B.** Be wary of a sudden gust
- **C.** Drive alongside very closely
- **D.** Expect normal conditions

Although motorcycles are more seriously affected, even motor cars can be blown off course by a sudden strong gust of wind. If you are travelling at 70mph, a slight change of direction might be enough to cause a serious accident.

Q 303 You could use the 'two-second rule'

Mark one answer

- **A.** Before restarting the engine after it's stalled
- **B.** To keep a safe gap from the vehicle in front
- **C.** Before using the 'mirror, signal, manoeuvre' routine
- **D.** When emerging on wet roads

Driving too close is a major cause of accidents. Here is a way to measure the **minimum** gap. Start saying 'Only a fool breaks the two-second rule!' when the vehicle in front of you passes a fixed position ahead. If you finish the rhyme before you reach that fixed position, you are keeping the minimum gap **for ideal driving conditions**.

Q 304 You are on a fast, open road in good conditions. For safety, the distance between you and the vehicle in front should be

Mark one answer

- **A.** A two-second time gap
- **B.** One car length
- **C.** 2 metres (6 feet 6 inches)
- **D.** Two car lengths

See **Q157** and **Q158**. The rhyme 'Only a fool breaks the two-second rule!' works for alert drivers in good conditions. It would not leave them enough space to pull up safely if the vehicle ahead stopped suddenly in bad conditions. Stopping distances are at least double on wet roads and up to ten times longer on icy roads.

Q 305 What does 'tailgating' mean?

Mark one answer

- [ ] **A.** When a vehicle delivering goods has its tailgate down
- [ ] **B.** When a vehicle is travelling with its back doors open
- [ ] **C.** When a driver is following another vehicle too closely
- [ ] **D.** When stationary vehicles are too close in a queue

Q 306 'Tailgating' means

Mark one answer

- [ ] **A.** Using the rear door of a hatchback car
- [ ] **B.** Reversing into a parking space
- [ ] **C.** Following another vehicle too closely
- [ ] **D.** Driving with rear fog lights on

> According to the two-second rule, there should be a gap of about 15 car lengths between two vehicles travelling at 70mph in the same direction on dry roads in good conditions. If the gap between two cars is only about two car lengths, the speed of the cars should be less than 10mph to avoid tailgating.

Q 307 The minimum safe time gap to keep between you and the vehicle in front in good conditions is at least

Mark one answer

- [ ] **A.** Four seconds
- [ ] **B.** One second
- [ ] **C.** Three seconds
- [ ] **D.** Two seconds

> The two-second rule applies to fit and healthy drivers who are alert and capable of responding quickly in an emergency. You should increase this minimum time gap if you really must drive when you are feeling tired or unwell.

Q 308 Stopping in good conditions at 30mph takes at least

Mark one answer

- [ ] **A.** Two car lengths
- [ ] **B.** Six car lengths
- [ ] **C.** Three car lengths
- [ ] **D.** One car length

Your overall stopping distance = your thinking distance + braking distance.

Speed	Thinking distance	Braking distance	Shortest stopping distance in metres
20 mph	6	6	12
30 mph	9	14	23
40 mph	12	24	36
50 mph	15	38	53
60 mph	18	55	73
70 mph	21	75	96

You should learn to judge your stopping distances when you are out in traffic.

Q 309 You are on a good, dry road surface and in a vehicle with good brakes and tyres. What is the shortest overall stopping distance at 40mph?

Mark one answer
- [ ] **A.** 23 metres (75 feet)
- [ ] **B.** 96 metres (315 feet)
- [ ] **C.** 53 metres (175 feet)
- [ ] **D.** 36 metres (120 feet)

Your thinking distance in feet is approximately the same number as your speed in mph. At 40mph your thinking distance is 40ft. To find your braking distance in feet you multiply your speed in mph (40) by its first figure (4) and divide the result (40 x 4 = 160) by 2 (160 ÷ 2 = 80). Add your thinking distance (40ft) to your braking distance (80ft) to get your shortest overall stopping distance: 120ft at 40mph.

Q 310 What is the braking distance at 50mph?

Mark one answer
- [ ] **A.** 55 metres (180 feet)
- [ ] **B.** 24 metres (79 feet)
- [ ] **C.** 14 metres (45 feet)
- [ ] **D.** 38 metres (125 feet)

To find the braking distance in feet, multiply the speed in mph (50) by its first figure (5) and divide the result (50 x 5 = 250) by 2 (250 ÷ 2 = 125ft).

Q 311 You are driving at 50mph in good conditions. What would be your shortest stopping distance?

Mark one answer
- [ ] **A.** 23 metres (75 feet)
- [ ] **B.** 36 metres (120 feet)
- [ ] **C.** 53 metres (175 feet)
- [ ] **D.** 73 metres (240 feet)

Thinking distance in feet is approximately the same number as the speed in mph. The shortest stopping distance at 50mph = thinking distance (50ft) + braking distance (125ft).

Q 312 You are travelling at 50mph on a good, dry road. What is your overall stopping distance?

Mark one answer
- [ ] **A.** 36 metres (120 feet)
- [ ] **B.** 53 metres (175 feet)
- [ ] **C.** 75 metres (245 feet)
- [ ] **D.** 96 metres (315 feet)

Q 313 What is the shortest overall stopping distance on a dry road from 60mph?

Mark one answer
- [ ] **A.** 53 metres (175 feet)
- [ ] **B.** 58 metres (190 feet)
- [ ] **C.** 73 metres (240 feet)
- [ ] **D.** 96 metres (315 feet)

Thinking distance = 60ft. Braking distance is (60 x 6) ÷ 2 = 180ft.
Shortest overall stopping distance = thinking distance + braking distance.

Q 314 What is the shortest stopping distance at 70mph?

Mark one answer
- [ ] **A.** 53 metres (175 feet)
- [ ] **B.** 60 metres (200 feet)
- [ ] **C.** 73 metres (240 feet)
- [ ] **D.** 96 metres (315 feet)

Thinking distance = 70ft. Braking distance is (70 x 7) ÷ 2 = 245ft.
Shortest overall stopping distance = thinking distance + braking distance.

Q 315 Your overall stopping distance will be much longer when driving

Mark one answer
- [ ] **A.** In the rain
- [ ] **B.** In fog
- [ ] **C.** At night
- [ ] **D.** In strong winds

On wet roads your stopping distances will be at least double what is required for dry roads.

Q 316 What is the main reason why your stopping distance is longer after heavy rain?

Mark one answer
- [ ] **A.** You may not be able to see large puddles
- [ ] **B.** The brakes will be cold because they're wet
- [ ] **C.** Your tyres will have less grip on the road
- [ ] **D.** Water on the windscreen will blur your view of the road ahead

Water makes road surfaces slippery and greatly increases stopping distances. Tyre tread pattern and depth are designed so your tyres can, for example, disperse up to 5 gallons (23 litres) of water per second and keep contact with the road at 60mph. Driving too fast with worn tyres on wet roads can cause aquaplaning. The tyres ride up on the water, lose their grip and cause the vehicle slide and skid. See **Q187**.

Q 317 You are driving in very wet weather. Your vehicle begins to slide. This effect is called

Mark one answer
- [ ] **A.** Hosing
- [ ] **B.** Weaving
- [ ] **C.** Aquaplaning
- [ ] **D.** Fading

The tread pattern and depth of tyres have to be capable of displacing 1 to 5 gallons (4.5–23 litres) of water per second so that the tyre can grip the wet road surface. Sensible drivers replace their tyres long before the tread wears down to the 1.6mm legal minimum.

Q 318 You are braking on a wet road. Your vehicle begins to skid and you do not have anti-lock brakes. What's the first thing you should do?

Mark one answer
- [ ] **A.** Quickly pull up the handbrake
- [ ] **B.** Push harder on the brake pedal
- [ ] **C.** Gently use the accelerator
- [ ] **D.** Release the footbrake fully

Q 319 You are braking on a wet road. Your vehicle begins to skid. Your vehicle does not have anti-lock brakes. What is the FIRST thing you should do?

Mark one answer

- **A.** Quickly pull up the handbrake
- **B.** Release the footbrake fully
- **C.** Push harder on the brake pedal
- **D.** Gently use the accelerator

In any skid, take your foot off the brake immediately. Keep a light grip on the steering wheel with both hands and leave the car in gear. See **Q190–Q192**. Remember that it is better to avoid a skid in the first place.

Q 320 You are turning left on a slippery road. The back of your vehicle slides to the right. What should you do?

Mark one answer

- **A.** Brake firmly and not turn the steering wheel
- **B.** Steer carefully to the right
- **C.** Steer carefully to the left
- **D.** Brake firmly and steer to the left

In a rear-wheel skid, steer left if the rear of the car is sliding to the left. Steer right if the rear of the car is sliding to the right. Do not oversteer. You could cause a skid in the opposite direction. In a front-wheel skid, release your accelerator pedal immediately and wait for your front tyres to regain some grip before trying to steer.

Q 321 You have driven through a flood. What is the first thing you should do?

Mark one answer

- **A.** Stop and check the tyres
- **B.** Stop and dry the brakes
- **C.** Switch on your windscreen wipers
- **D.** Test your brakes

Your brakes may fail if water gets onto the friction material of the drum linings or brake pads. Testing your brakes in wet conditions will help to dry them out and restore their efficiency. See **Q193**, **Q194** and **Q555**.

Q 322 Braking distances on ice can be

Mark one answer

- **A.** Twice the normal distance
- **B.** Five times the normal distance
- **C.** Seven times the normal distance
- **D.** Ten times the normal distance

Driving in snow and on ice is extremely dangerous. You face the constant risk of the wheels spinning or locking. Drive slowly in the highest gear possible. Steer smoothly. Use engine braking and try to avoid touching the brake pedal, especially on corners.

Q 323 You are driving on an icy road. What distance should you drive from the car in front?

Mark one answer
- [ ] **A.** Eight times the normal distance
- [ ] **B.** Six times the normal distance
- [ ] **C.** Ten times the normal distance
- [ ] **D.** Four times the normal distance

According to the two-second rule, there should be a gap of about 3 car lengths between two vehicles travelling at 15mph in the same direction on good, dry roads. If the roads are icy, there should be a gap of about 30 car lengths!

Q 324 Freezing conditions will affect the distance it takes you to come to a stop. You should expect stopping distances to increase by up to

Mark one answer
- [ ] **A.** Two times
- [ ] **B.** Five times
- [ ] **C.** Three times
- [ ] **D.** Ten times

If you touch the brake pedal, you must do so extremely gently when driving on icy roads. The wheels can easily lock so that you lose control of your steering and begin to skid.

Q 325 How can you tell when you are driving over black ice?

Mark one answer
- [ ] **A.** It is easier to brake
- [ ] **B.** The noise from your tyres sounds louder
- [ ] **C.** You see black ice on the road
- [ ] **D.** Your steering feels light
- [ ] **E.** Other vehicles will get out of the way

One problem with 'black ice' is that you are usually unaware of it until your steering begins to feel light. If you are driving too fast for the conditions this warning comes too late. Do remember that it is better to avoid a skid than to have to deal with one.

Q 326 When driving in icy conditions, the steering becomes light because the tyres

Mark one answer
- [ ] **A.** Have more grip on the road
- [ ] **B.** Are too soft
- [ ] **C.** Are too hard
- [ ] **D.** Have less grip on the road

Always keep your tyres inflated to the pressures recommended by the manufacturer. Do not lower the pressure for icy conditions. You will not improve their grip, but you *will* increase the risk of damage to their walls.

Q 327 You are driving in heavy rain when your steering suddenly becomes very light. To get control again you must

Mark one answer
- [ ] **A.** Brake firmly to reduce speed
- [ ] **B.** Ease off the accelerator
- [ ] **C.** Use the accelerator gently
- [ ] **D.** Steer towards a dry part of the road

You apply engine braking when you take your foot off the accelerator pedal. The lower the gear you are in the greater the engine braking. Easing off the accelerator is the first step in any progressive braking routine.

Q 328 How can you avoid wheelspin when driving in freezing conditions?

Mark one answer

[ ] **A.** Stay in first gear all the time
[ ] **B.** Put on your handbrake if the wheels begin to slip
[ ] **C.** Drive in as high a gear as possible
[ ] **D.** Allow the vehicle to coast in neutral

The engine supplies the greatest power to the wheels when the vehicle is in its lowest gear. This is why you normally use the lowest gear when moving off and keep in a low gear when climbing hills. Less power is needed for driving at a constant speed on a level road so then you use a high gear. On icy roads you need gentle acceleration so the wheels turn slowly.

Q 329 You are driving on an icy road. How can you avoid wheel spin?

Mark one answer

[ ] **A.** Drive at a slow speed in as high a gear as possible
[ ] **B.** Use the handbrake if the wheels start to slip
[ ] **C.** Brake gently and repeatedly
[ ] **D.** Drive in a low gear at all times

On icy roads you want to avoid wheel spin and wheel lock. You risk wheel spin by harsh acceleration in low gear. You risk locking the wheels by harsh braking in any gear. Remember that you apply the handbrake to set the rear brakes and only after you have stopped moving.

Q 330 When snow is falling heavily you should

Mark one answer

[ ] **A.** Drive as long as your headlights are used
[ ] **B.** Not drive unless you have a mobile phone
[ ] **C.** Drive only when your journey is short
[ ] **D.** Not drive unless it's essential

Q 331 When driving in snow it is best to keep in as high a gear as possible. Why is this?

Mark one answer

[ ] **A.** To help you slow down quickly when you brake
[ ] **B.** So that wheel spin does not cause your engine to run too fast
[ ] **C.** To leave a lower gear available in case of wheel spin
[ ] **D.** To help to prevent wheel spin

See **Q330** and **Q331** above.

Q 332 You are turning left on a slippery road. The back of your vehicle slides to the right. You should

Mark one answer

[ ] **A.** Brake firmly and not turn the steering wheel
[ ] **B.** Steer carefully to the left
[ ] **C.** Steer carefully to the right
[ ] **D.** Brake firmly and steer to the left

Q 333 You are driving in freezing conditions. Which TWO should you do when approaching a sharp bend?

Mark two answers
- [ ] **A.** Accelerate into the bend
- [ ] **B.** Slow down before you reach the bend
- [ ] **C.** Gently apply your handbrake
- [ ] **D.** Avoid sudden steering movements
- [ ] **E.** Position towards the middle of the road

On icy roads avoid sudden changes of speed and/or direction. Take your foot off the accelerator to let engine braking gently slow your vehicle **before** you reach any bend or corner.

Q 334 When driving in fog in daylight you should use

Mark one answer
- [ ] **A.** Sidelights
- [ ] **B.** Full beam headlights
- [ ] **C.** Hazard lights
- [ ] **D.** Dipped headlights

See **Q207** to **Q219** inclusive.

Q 335 What TWO safeguards could you take against fire risk to your vehicle?

Mark two answers
- [ ] **A.** Keep water levels above maximum
- [ ] **B.** Carry a fire extinguisher
- [ ] **C.** Avoid driving with a full tank of petrol
- [ ] **D.** Use unleaded petrol
- [ ] **E.** Check out any strong smell of petrol
- [ ] **F.** Use low octane fuel

There is always a serious risk of fire and explosion if petrol or its vapour leaks out. When you are refuelling do not let your tank overflow. Stop refuelling when the trigger in the nozzle of the petrol pump cuts out automatically. If the event of fire, keep people at a safe distance. Do not put water on to burning fuel. Use a dry powder or foam extinguisher. If you cannot control the fire at its outbreak, keep clear and wait for the fire brigade.

Q 336 A tanker is involved in an accident. Which sign would show if the tanker is carrying dangerous goods?

Mark one answer

- [ ] **A.**  **LONG VEHICLE**

- [ ] **B.**

- [ ] **C.**

- [ ] **D.**

The emergency services need to know how dangerous the chemicals are. An information panel on the lorry may tell them whether the chemicals are toxic, corrosive, flammable, radioactive, etc. A telephone number on the panel lets them call someone who can give them further information about the lorry and its load. You can find an illustration of a panel and some hazard warning symbols in The Highway Code.

Q 337 You arrive at the scene of a motorcycle accident. The rider is conscious but in shock. You should make sure that

Mark one answer
- **A.** The rider's helmet is removed
- **B.** The rider is moved to the side of the road
- **C.** The rider's helmet is not removed
- **D.** The rider is put in the recovery position

You should not remove a rider's helmet unless he or she has stopped breathing and you cannot begin resuscitation if the helmet is left on. Clear the casualty's mouth of any obvious obstruction and tilt the head back. If breathing does not begin spontaneously, pinch the casualty's nose and blow into the mouth until the chest rises. Stop and repeat the procedure once every 4 seconds until the casualty can breath unaided.

Q 338 You arrive at the scene of a motorcycle accident. No other vehicle is involved. The rider is unconscious, lying in the middle of the road. The first thing you should do is

Mark one answer
- **A.** Move the rider out of the road
- **B.** Warn other traffic
- **C.** Clear the road of debris
- **D.** Give the rider reassurance

The law requires drivers to stop if they are the first to arrive on the scene. See **Q339** and **Q340**.

Q 339 You have stopped at the scene of an accident to give help. Which THREE things should you do?

Mark three answers
- **A.** Keep injured people warm and comfortable
- **B.** Keep injured people calm by talking to them reassuringly
- **C.** Keep injured people on the move by walking them around
- **D.** Give injured people a warm drink
- **E.** Make sure that injured people are not left alone

Never give casualties anything to drink. Never move casualties unless they are in danger. If you attempt to move a casualty you may make their injuries worse.

Q 340 You are the first person to arrive at an accident where people are badly injured. Which THREE should you do?

Mark three answers
- **A.** Switch on your own hazard warning lights
- **B.** Make sure that someone telephones for an ambulance
- **C.** Try and get people who are injured to drink something
- **D.** Move the people who are injured clear of their vehicles
- **E.** Get people who are not injured clear of the scene

If you are the first to arrive at the scene of an accident, stop and switch on your hazard lights to warn others. Send for the emergency services. Set up a warning triangle. Switch off engines and stop anyone smoking. Try to minimise the risk of fire and further collisions. Do not move casualties unless they are in danger, but get any uninjured people clear of the scene. See **Q338** and **Q339**.

Q 341 You are the first to arrive at the scene of an accident. Which FOUR of these should you do?

Mark four answers

- [ ] **A.** Leave as soon as another motorist arrives
- [ ] **B.** Switch off the vehicle engine(s)
- [ ] **C.** Move uninjured people away from the vehicle(s)
- [ ] **D.** Call the emergency services
- [ ] **E.** Warn other traffic

You should not leave the scene of an accident until the emergency services have arrived and, if appropriate, you have given details to anyone with reasonable grounds for requiring them.

Q 342 You are involved in a road accident with another driver. Your vehicle is damaged. Which FOUR of the following should you find out?

Mark four answers

- [ ] **A.** Whether the driver owns the other vehicle involved
- [ ] **B.** The other driver's name, address and telephone number
- [ ] **C.** The car make and registration number of the other vehicle
- [ ] **D.** The occupation of the other driver
- [ ] **E.** The details of the other driver's vehicle insurance
- [ ] **F.** Whether the other driver is licensed to drive

At an accident you must provide your name, address and other details to anyone having reasonable grounds for requiring them. Your insurance company expects you to notify it of any accident even if you are not to blame and you are not making a claim. Make sure you know and follow your insurance company's advice on what to do if you are involved in an accident.

Q 343 You have an accident while driving and someone is injured. You do not produce your insurance certificate at the time. You must report it to the police as soon as possible, or in any case within

Mark one answer

- [ ] **A.** 24 hours
- [ ] **B.** 48 hours
- [ ] **C.** Five days
- [ ] **D.** Seven days

The same requirements about providing details apply if you do not injure a person but you cause damage to property, or you injure a dog, ass, mule, pig, goat, sheep, horse or cow. You must report the accident to the police as soon as possible.

Q 344 You are in an accident on an 'A' class road. You have a warning triangle with you. At what distance before the obstruction should you place the warning triangle?

Mark one answer

- [ ] **A.** 100 metres (330 feet)
- [ ] **B.** 50 metres (165 feet)
- [ ] **C.** 25 metres (80 feet)
- [ ] **D.** 150 metres (492 feet)

Accidents usually cause an obstruction. Then there is the danger of other vehicles colliding into the accident scene. A triangle should warn traffic of danger ahead so there is enough time to take appropriate action.

Q 345 You have broken down on a two-way road. You have a warning triangle. You should place the warning triangle at least how far from your vehicle?

Mark one answer
- **A.** 5 metres (16 feet)
- **B.** 25 metres (80 feet)
- **C.** 50 metres (165 feet)
- **D.** 100 metres (330 feet)

If you break down on a motorway you should, if possible, place a warning triangle on the hard shoulder 150m (492ft) back from your vehicle to alert other drivers. **Never** attempt to put a warning triangle on the carriageway.

Q 346 You have broken down on an ordinary road. You have a warning triangle. It should be displayed

Mark one answer
- **A.** On the roof of your vehicle
- **B.** At least 150 metres (492 feet) behind your vehicle
- **C.** At least 50 metres (165 feet) behind your vehicle
- **D.** Just behind your vehicle

Remember to place the triangle on the same side of road as the obstruction. This is usually on the left-hand side of the street and facing the traffic approaching your vehicle. Where should you put it if your vehicle has broken down in a one-way street?

Q 347 When are you allowed to use hazard warning lights?

Mark one answer
- **A.** When stopped and temporarily obstructing traffic
- **B.** When driving during darkness without headlights
- **C.** When parked for shopping on double yellow lines
- **D.** When travelling slowly because you are lost

See **Q266**, **Q267** and **Q482**. Hazard warning lights are for real emergencies only. Your vehicle must not be moving unless you are on a motorway or unrestricted dual carriageway and warning drivers behind you of danger ahead. The use of hazard warning lights does not authorise you to park illegally or ignore parking restrictions.

Q 348 When should you switch on your hazard warning lights?

Mark one answer

☐ **A.** When you cannot avoid causing an obstruction

☐ **B.** When you are driving slowly due to bad weather

☐ **C.** When you are towing a broken down vehicle

☐ **D.** When you are parked on double yellow lines

If your vehicle breaks down, get it off the road as soon as possible so that it does not obstruct other traffic. Get your vehicle on to the hard shoulder if you have a breakdown on the motorway.

Q 349 For which TWO should you use hazard warning lights?

Mark two answers

☐ **A.** When you slow down quickly on a motorway because of a hazard ahead

☐ **B.** When you have broken down

☐ **C.** When you wish to stop on double yellow lines

☐ **D.** When you need to park on the pavement

See **Q348** and **Q350**.

Q 350 For which THREE should you use your hazard warning lights?

Mark three answers

☐ **A.** When you are parking in a restricted area

☐ **B.** When you are temporarily obstructing traffic

☐ **C.** To warn following traffic of a hazard ahead

☐ **D.** When you have broken down

You warn other road users of a hazard or a temporary obstruction when you switch on all four indicator lights to flash at the same time. It is an offence to use hazard warning lights other than in an emergency. See **Q266** and **Q267**.

Q 351 You are on the motorway. Luggage falls from your vehicle. What should you do?

Mark one answer

☐ **A.** Stop at the next emergency telephone and contact the police

☐ **B.** Stop on the motorway and put on hazard lights whilst you pick it up

☐ **C.** Reverse back up the motorway to pick it up

☐ **D.** Pull up on the hard shoulder and wave traffic down

It is an offence to cause danger by carrying an insecure load. Luggage on your roof rack will increase fuel consumption and running costs. It may make your car less stable. If you overload the roof rack, your insurance company could refuse your claim for damage or loss. See **Q225** and **Q226**.

Q 352 You are driving on a motorway. A large box falls on to the carriageway from a lorry ahead of you. The lorry does not stop. You should

Mark one answer

- [ ] **A.** Drive to the next emergency telephone and inform the police
- [ ] **B.** Catch up with the lorry and try to get the driver's attention
- [ ] **C.** Stop close to the box and switch on your hazard warning lights until the police arrive
- [ ] **D.** Pull over to the hard shoulder, then try and remove the box

> Motorways are extremely dangerous places for stationary vehicles and pedestrians even on the hard shoulder. You will find a free-call telephone at one-mile intervals along the hard shoulder so you can contact the emergency services. If you have to stop because you cannot change lanes to avoid the box, you must switch on your hazard warning lights to alert traffic following behind you. Use your car telephone, if you have one, to contact the emergency services.

Q 353 Your vehicle has a puncture on a motorway. What should you do?

Mark one answer

- [ ] **A.** Drive slowly to the next service area to get assistance
- [ ] **B.** Pull up on the hard shoulder. Change the wheel as quickly as possible
- [ ] **C.** Pull up on the hard shoulder. Use the emergency phone to get assistance
- [ ] **D.** Switch on your hazard lights. Stop in your lane

> Even if you have put up a warning triangle 150m (492ft) back on the hard shoulder and even if you are capable of changing a wheel yourself, you must call the emergency services. The police need to know your position in order to deal with the potential dangers of the situation. They have to protect you and other motorway users. See **Q442** and **Q478**.

Q 354 Your tyre bursts while you are driving. Which TWO things should you do?

Mark two answers

- [ ] **A.** Pull on the handbrake
- [ ] **B.** Brake as quickly as possible
- [ ] **C.** Pull up slowly at the side of the road
- [ ] **D.** Hold the steering wheel firmly to keep control
- [ ] **E.** Continue on at a normal speed

> If a tyre bursts you will feel the steering become heavy. Your car may become difficult to control and tend to slew off the road when you brake. Remember it is an offence to drive on tyres which are under-inflated. And driving on a flat tyre even for a short distance can damage it beyond repair. Find a safe place and change the wheel as soon as possible.

Q 355 Which TWO things should you do when a front tyre bursts?

Mark two answers

- [ ] **A.** Apply the handbrake to stop the vehicle
- [ ] **B.** Brake firmly and quickly
- [ ] **C.** Let the vehicle roll to a stop
- [ ] **D.** Hold the steering wheel lightly
- [ ] **E.** Grip the steering wheel firmly

> If you press the brake pedal when a tyre bursts, you could lose control and slew off the road. You should take firm hold of the steering wheel with both hands to keep the vehicle under control. At the same time, keep off the accelerator and brake pedal so that engine braking can occur.

Q 356 At a railway level crossing the red light signal continues to flash after a train has gone by. What should you do?

Mark one answer
- **A.** Phone the signal operator
- **B.** Alert drivers behind you
- **C.** Wait
- **D.** Proceed with caution

Trains always have priority where the track crosses a road. A flashing red light signals the approach of one or more trains. You **must stop** behind the white line in front of the barrier. Be a patient driver not a hospital patient. See **Q436**.

Q 357 You have stalled in the middle of a level crossing and cannot restart the engine. The warning bell starts to ring. You should

Mark one answer
- **A.** Get out and clear of the crossing
- **B.** Run down the track to warn the signalman
- **C.** Carry on trying to restart the engine
- **D.** Push the vehicle clear of the crossing

After the warning bell starts ringing, the barriers come down to keep the track clear for the trains about to arrive. In these circumstances, your first priority is get yourself clear of the crossing. Remember that you can avoid stalling on a crossing by driving on to it only when your way forward is clear for you to cross it completely. See **Q358** and **Q359**.

Q 358 Your vehicle has broken down on an automatic railway level crossing. What should you do FIRST?

Mark one answer
- **A.** Get everyone out of the vehicle and clear of the crossing
- **B.** Phone the signal operator so that trains can be stopped
- **C.** Walk along the track to give warning to any approaching trains
- **D.** Try to push the vehicle clear of the crossing as soon as possible

Preventing injury to yourself and others should take priority over avoiding damage to property. When everyone is clear of the crossing, you need immediately to contact the signal operator to warn of danger to the trains. Then follow any instructions the operator may give you. If there are no warnings of trains expected, you may have time to try moving your vehicle off the crossing.

Q 359 You break down on a level crossing. The lights have not yet begun to flash. Which THREE things should you do?

Mark three answers
- **A.** Telephone the signal operator
- **B.** Leave your vehicle and get everyone clear
- **C.** Walk down the track and signal the next train
- **D.** Move the vehicle if a signal operator tells you to
- **E.** Tell drivers behind what has happened

If you unavoidably break down on a crossing, you must take the following steps promptly and in order:
1. move yourself and others clear of the crossing
2. make telephone contact with the signal operator
3. follow any instructions the signal operator gives you

The four topics in this section are about **motoring regulations** and **laws.** The first topic is about documents required for using vehicles. The next two topics are about regulations for roads and motorways. The fourth topic deals with traffic signs, road markings, signals, speed limits, priority and rights of way.

DOCUMENTS

By law you require a **driving licence** (signed and valid for your vehicle), a **vehicle excise licence** (current tax disc displayed on the vehicle) and **third party insurance** (against liability for damage to property and injury to other people including passengers). Driving without this minimum insurance is a very serious offence. You are not required by law to carry insurance for fire, theft or personal injury even though many sensible people do. If your motor car is over three years old you also require a current **test certificate** (MOT).

RULES OF THE ROAD

Speed limits

A speed limit is a maximum, **not** a target. Speed limits depend on the type of road and the type of vehicle. A limit of 30mph is normal in built up areas. When there are no street lamps at frequent intervals, speed limit signs are displayed. Remember that speeds under 30mph may still be too fast for many road and traffic conditions. Limits of 40mph often apply near the edges of towns and on dual carriageways where repeater speed limit signs are displayed and traffic may flow faster. Good drivers try to keep up with the flow of traffic but without breaking the speed limit.

The national speed limit for single-carriageway roads is 60mph. When it applies in rural areas there are usually no signs or street lamps. When the national speed limit applies in urban areas there are repeater signs displayed. The maximum speed limit on dual carriageways is 70mph. When the limit on a rural road or a dual carriageway is restricted to 50mph, watch out for additional hazards such as dangerous junctions, unexpected traffic lights or pedestrians crossing.

Parking and lighting

We do not have an automatic right to park on the roads. By law they are 'for the purpose of passage'. To keep within the law we should either get permission from a uniformed police officer (or traffic warden) or use an authorised parking place such as a parking meter bay. If you park in an unauthorised place you could be charged with dangerous parking, obstruction and other illegal parking offences. You are causing an obstruction if you park your car on a pavement or grass verge. Leaving your car on the wrong side of the road after dark is dangerous parking. Check The Highway Code for precise details on parking regulations, but in general the rules are quite clear.

MOTORWAY RULES

The maximum speed limit on motorways is 70mph for motorcycles, cars, buses and coaches. It is 60mph for articulated goods vehicles, those towing a trailer or those exceeding 7.5 tonnes. The maximum speed limit is also 60mph if your car is towing a caravan or trailer.

Motorway traffic is one-way. You must never reverse, drive against the traffic flow or cross the central reservation. Keep in the left lane. Overtake only on the right unless traffic is moving slowly in queues. Do not use the right-hand lane of a three-lane motorway if your vehicle is towing a caravan or trailer. You must not stop on the motorway (and slipways) except in an emergency and then only on the hard shoulder. Being in need of sleep is **not** an emergency according to the law.

ROAD AND TRAFFIC SIGNS

Signals, signs and road markings all help to keep traffic flowing safely but only if you see and act upon them correctly.

Traffic signs

You need to understand the basic shapes and diagrams on the signs. The colours are not essential but they do make the signs clearer. The red STOP sign has the octagon shape and means you must stop at the line. The

GIVE WAY sign has the upside down triangle shape. It warns you to be prepared to stop at the STOP sign or to give way at the GIVE WAY sign. Both signs are extremely important and easily recognised. Other signs giving orders are mostly circular. Blue means a positive order (**do**). Red means a negative order (**don't**). Warning signs are mostly triangles with a red border. You should heed the warning even though you need not obey the sign. Information and direction signs are rectangular with a blue background for motorway signs and a green background for primary route signs.

Road markings

White lines along the middle of the road separate traffic travelling in opposite directions and warn you of additional danger. More white paint means more danger. There are restrictions on parking, stopping and waiting alongside double white lines even if one of the lines is broken.

Do not straddle or cross

- a **single broken** line, with long markings and short gaps, unless you can plainly see that the road is clear well ahead
- a **double white** line except from the broken line side and unless it is safe to do so
- a **double solid white** line from either direction except in an emergency

It is extremely dangerous to cross a double white line but you may do so to get in and out of premises, to avoid a stationary obstruction or to turn into a side road. It is illegal to straddle or cross a double solid white line in order to overtake an obstruction travelling at less than 10mph unless it is a horse and rider, a pedal cyclist or a road maintenance vehicle. Note that slow-moving tractors are not road maintenance vehicles!

Parking restrictions are indicated by yellow lines at the roadside (red lines in London) and loading/unloading restrictions are marked by yellow lines on the kerb. More yellow paint means less parking and waiting because there is more danger. Zigzag markings warn you of dangers at pedestrian crossings and school entrances, where you must not stop to load or unload goods or passengers. Parking, stopping and waiting regulations apply alongside double white lines even if one is broken and even without yellow lines at the kerbside.

Traffic lights

You must know the sequence of the signals at traffic lights and pedestrian crossings. Red means stop. Green means go only if the way forward is clear, so you must take care when approaching a green light. The amber light means stop. Never cross it except in the emergency situation of avoiding an accident with another vehicle.

Signals by authorised persons

Uniformed police officers are authorised to control traffic. They use their right arm to signal to traffic approaching them from the front. Their left arm is for traffic coming from behind. They keep their arms still to stop the traffic. They move their arms to wave traffic on. A police officer's signals can override any other traffic controls and must be obeyed. Traffic wardens have the same authority as police to control traffic and use the same arm signals. School crossing patrols are authorised to assist children crossing roads on their way to and from schools. You must stop your vehicle when a crossing patrol shows you the STOP – CHILDREN sign. Traffic signs operated by workmen have the same meanings as any other traffic lights. A person in charge of animals is also allowed to control traffic. If a traffic controller directs you to cross a hazard warning line, it is still your responsibility to do so safely.

Q 360 To drive on the road learners MUST

Mark one answer

- [ ] **A.** Have NO penalty points on their licence
- [ ] **B.** Have taken professional instruction
- [ ] **C.** Have a signed, valid provisional licence
- [ ] **D.** Apply for a driving test within 12 months

It is important to have lessons with a qualified professional instructor as soon as you decide to learn to drive and certainly before you ever sit in a driving seat to take hold of a steering wheel. It will be quicker and cheaper in the long run. Remember that you are learning a life skill. You can all too easily acquire from well-meaning, unqualified amateurs the wrong attitude and bad habits that could prove expensive and even cost you your life. And by the way, don't forget that the law treats provisional licence-holders no differently from full licence-holders. Motoring offences are criminal offences carrying punishments. See **Q73**.

Q 361 Your driving licence must be signed by

Mark one answer

- [ ] **A.** A police officer
- [ ] **B.** A driving instructor
- [ ] **C.** Your next of kin
- [ ] **D.** You

When you receive your licence, you should check the details and sign it. If you do not sign your licence it will not be valid. When you have completed your course of professional instruction and passed your test, the same will apply to the full driving licence you are granted. Remember that you must also be medically fit to drive. An undisclosed disability could invalidate your licence.

Q 362 As a provisional licence-holder you should not drive a car

Mark one answer

- [ ] **A.** Over 50mph
- [ ] **B.** At night
- [ ] **C.** On the motorway
- [ ] **D.** With passengers in rear seats

In a complete course of lessons, a fully qualified professional instructor would expect to teach you how to drive on dual carriageways at 70mph before you take your practical test and how to drive on motorways after you pass your test.

Q 363 Which THREE of the following do you need before you can drive legally?

Mark three answers

- [ ] **A.** A valid signed driving licence
- [ ] **B.** A valid tax disc displayed on your vehicle
- [ ] **C.** Proof of your identity
- [ ] **D.** A current MOT certificate if the car is over three years old (or four years in Northern Ireland)
- [ ] **E.** Fully comprehensive insurance
- [ ] **F.** A vehicle handbook

You must display a valid tax disc as proof that you have paid your vehicle excise licence fee. Remember that a current MOT certificate is no guarantee that your vehicle is in a roadworthy condition. Always do your routine daily and weekly checks. Be sure your vehicle is serviced properly and regularly.

Q 364 Before driving anyone else's motor vehicle you should make sure that

Mark one answer

- [ ] **A.** The vehicle owner has third party insurance cover
- [ ] **B.** Your own vehicle has insurance cover
- [ ] **C.** The vehicle is insured for your use
- [ ] **D.** The owner has left the insurance documents in the vehicle

> You must never drive a vehicle unless it is insured for you to use. Driving without insurance is a serious offence which could lead to possible disqualification and a fine of up to £5000. Your own car insurance may cover you to drive other cars. Remember that your insurance for other cars may be third party only. It may not cover damage to this other car you are driving even if it gives comprehensive cover for your own car.

Q 365 What is the legal minimum insurance cover you must have to drive on public roads?

Mark one answer

- [ ] **A.** Third party, fire and theft
- [ ] **B.** Fully comprehensive
- [ ] **C.** Third party only
- [ ] **D.** Personal injury cover

> By law, your vehicle must be properly insured to cover against third party and passenger liability. This means your vehicle is insured against any claim by passengers or other persons for damage or injury to their person or property. It usually costs very little more for third party, fire & theft insurance to cover your own vehicle against damage by fire and loss by theft.

Q 366 Your car has third party insurance. What does this cover?

Mark three answers

- [ ] **A.** Damage to your own car
- [ ] **B.** Damage to your car by fire
- [ ] **C.** Injury to another person
- [ ] **D.** Damage to someone else's property
- [ ] **E.** Damage to other vehicles
- [ ] **F.** Injury to yourself

> You should think seriously about including personal injury insurance in your cover.

Q 367 The cost of your insurance will be reduced if

Mark one answer

- [ ] **A.** Your car is large and powerful
- [ ] **B.** You are using the car for work purposes
- [ ] **C.** You have penalty points on your licence
- [ ] **D.** You are over 25 years old

> The cost of your motor insurance depends the type of insurance (fully comprehensive is the most expensive), the type and size of your vehicle and the power of its engine, where you live, how old you are, how long you have held a full licence and your accident record. See **Q127, Q129** and **Q131**.

Q 368 For which TWO of these must you show your motor insurance certificate?

Mark two answers

- [ ] **A.** When you are taking your driving test
- [ ] **B.** When buying or selling a vehicle
- [ ] **C.** When a police officer asks you for it
- [ ] **D.** When you are taxing your vehicle
- [ ] **E.** When having an MOT inspection

You cannot tax a vehicle that is uninsured. Driving without insurance is a very serious offence that the DVLA cannot condone. If you are involved in an accident causing injury, you will be required to show the police your valid motor insurance certificate.

Q 369 Motor cars and motorcycles must FIRST have an MOT test certificate when they are

Mark one answer
- [ ] **A.** One year old
- [ ] **B.** Three years old
- [ ] **C.** Five years old
- [ ] **D.** Seven years old

An MOT certificate relates only to the condition of the items examined on the day of the test. It does not cover the condition of the engine, clutch or gearbox. The certificate is valid for 12 months but does not confirm that the vehicle will remain roadworthy for that period of time. You can apply for a new certificate not more than one month before the old one expires. If you produce your old certificate when your new one is being issued, the new expiry date may be entered as 12 months from the expiry date of the old certificate.

Q 370 An MOT certificate is normally valid for

Mark one answer
- [ ] **A.** Three years after the date it was issued
- [ ] **B.** 10,000 miles
- [ ] **C.** One year after the date it was issued
- [ ] **D.** 30,000 miles

See **Q369** above.

Q 371 Your vehicle needs a current MOT certificate. You do not have one. Until you do have one you will not be able to renew your

Mark one answer
- [ ] **A.** Driving licence
- [ ] **B.** Vehicle insurance
- [ ] **C.** Road tax disc
- [ ] **D.** Vehicle registration document

You do not need to drive or own a car in order to have a driving licence. However, before you drive a vehicle on the public highway it must be registered, taxed and properly insured.

Q 372 When is it legal to drive a car over three years old without an MOT certificate?

Mark one answer
- [ ] **A.** Up to seven days after the old certificate has run out
- [ ] **B.** When driving to an MOT centre to arrange an appointment
- [ ] **C.** Just after buying a second-hand car with no MOT
- [ ] **D.** When driving to an appointment at an MOT centre

It is an offence to drive a car that is not roadworthy. It is also an offence to drive a roadworthy car without a valid MOT certificate if that car is more than 3 years old. The only exception is when driving to an authorised MOT test centre for an examination booked in advanced.

Q 373 Which of these vehicles is not required to have an MOT certificate?

Mark two answers
- [ ] **A.** Police vehicle
- [ ] **B.** Small trailer
- [ ] **C.** Ambulance
- [ ] **D.** Taxi
- [ ] **E.** Caravan

> Caravans and trailers must be roadworthy and comply with the Road Vehicles (Construction and Use) Regulations laid down by acts of law. These regulations cover brakes, lighting, tyres, etc. Remember that the rear of the caravan must display the licence plate of the vehicle towing it.

Mark three answers
- [ ] **A.** Registered keeper
- [ ] **B.** Make of the vehicle
- [ ] **C.** Service history details
- [ ] **D.** Date of the MOT
- [ ] **E.** Type of insurance cover
- [ ] **F.** Engine size

> You should keep your vehicle registration document in a safe place – **never in the vehicle**. You are required by law to notify the DVLA (Driver and Vehicle Licensing Authority) of any changes to the name and address or vehicle particulars printed on the document as soon as they occur. It is an offence to alter or obliterate any details in the document or to supply false information for the purpose of registration.

Q 374 A police officer asks to see your driving documents. You do not have them with you. You may produce them at a police station within

Mark one answer
- [ ] **A.** 5 days
- [ ] **B.** 7 days
- [ ] **C.** 14 days
- [ ] **D.** 21 days

> It may be convenient to carry around your motor insurance certificate with you your driving licence. It is neither wise nor safe ever to leave the certificate in your vehicle. You may find your licence accepted by people in various organisations who require some form of identification. By law, however, you are only required to show your licence to a police officer in uniform when it is requested.

Q 376 A friend wants to teach you to drive a car. They must

Mark one answer
- [ ] **A.** Be over 21 and have held a full licence for at least two years
- [ ] **B.** Be over 18 and hold an advanced driver's certificate
- [ ] **C.** Be over 18 and have fully comprehensive insurance
- [ ] **D.** Be over 21 and have held a full licence for at least three years

> There is no substitute for proper lessons from a fully qualified driving instructor approved by the Department of Transport. There is also no substitute for good experience gained through proper practice. Anyone supervising learner drivers must hold a full UK licence valid for the category of vehicle being driven by the learner. Your instructor should arrange for any would-be supervising relative or friend to attend one of your lessons. The instructor can make both of you aware of the legal responsibilities and conditions that apply to you and to anyone supervising you. See **Q360**.

Q 375 Which THREE pieces of information are found on a vehicle registration document?

Q 377 In which TWO places must you NOT park?

Mark two answers
- [ ] **A.** Near a school entrance
- [ ] **B.** Near a police station
- [ ] **C.** In a side road
- [ ] **D.** At a bus stop
- [ ] **E.** In a one-way street

When you park on a road your vehicle restricts the width of road available to other traffic. It is also an obstruction which can hide pedestrians from the view of oncoming drivers. If you park near a bus stop you may add to the bus driver's difficulties in manoeuvring a large vehicle. If you park near a school you may add to the children's difficulties in crossing the road safely.

Q 378 In which THREE places must you NEVER park your vehicle?

Mark three answers
- [ ] **A.** Near the brow of a hill
- [ ] **B.** At or near a bus stop
- [ ] **C.** Where there is no pavement
- [ ] **D.** Within 10 metres (33 feet) of a junction
- [ ] **E.** On a 40mph road

Aound 75% of all accidents occur on built-up roads. More than two-thirds of these occur at or near junctions. Turning out of a junction can be difficult and dangerous. Vehicles parked close to the junction can make it even more difficult and dangerous. The vehicles may seriously restrict the width of the road and the view available to road users. You must not park opposite double white hazard warning lines, even if one of them is a broken line.

Q 379 In which FOUR places must you NOT park or wait?

Mark four answers
- [ ] **A.** On a dual carriageway
- [ ] **B.** At a bus stop
- [ ] **C.** On the slope of a hill
- [ ] **D.** Opposite a traffic island
- [ ] **E.** In front of someone else's drive
- [ ] **F.** On the brow of a hill

Always think carefully about where to stop, wait or park. Do not obstruct the passage of other road users, especially if they are put at risk trying to avoid your vehicle. Traffic islands are often safe places in the road for pedestrians waiting to use a crossing. Remember that it is an offence to park within the area marked by the zigzag lines of a crossing.

Q 380 At which of these places are you **sometimes** allowed to park your vehicle?

Mark one answer
- [ ] **A.** On the nearside lane of a motorway
- [ ] **B.** On a clearway
- [ ] **C.** Where there is a single broken yellow line
- [ ] **D.** On the zigzag lines of a zebra crossing

Always check the small print on the restriction plates and parking notices where yellow line parking restrictions are in force. It is also sensible to find, if possible, the particular reasons for any restrictions. Continuous single or double yellow lines warn you of severe restrictions on parking and waiting. See **Q31, Q136, Q137** and **Q599**.

Q 381 You are looking for somewhere to park your vehicle. The area is full EXCEPT for spaces marked 'disabled use'. You must

Mark one answer

- **A.** Use these spaces when elsewhere is full
- **B.** Stay with your vehicle when you park there
- **C.** Use these spaces, disabled or not
- **D.** Not park there unless permitted

A traffic warden can fine you for parking without permission in a disabled space set aside by the local authority. These spaces are often the ones closest to a shopping centre or public utilities so that someone who is disabled has less distance to walk than an able-bodied person.

Q 382 What MUST you have to park in a disabled space?

Mark one answer

- **A.** An orange badge
- **B.** A wheelchair
- **C.** An advanced driver certificate
- **D.** A modified vehicle

The local authority usually issue the parking permits for drivers (or passengers) with disabilities to use in the area where they normally live. Different local councils and city authorities have their own special rules. The official permit must be displayed like the tax disc in the windscreen. You should not confuse it with the disabled person stickers you sometimes see in car rear windows!

Q 383 What is the nearest you may park your vehicle to a junction?

Mark one answer

- **A.** 10 metres (33 feet)
- **B.** 12 metres (40 feet)
- **C.** 15 metres (50 feet)
- **D.** 20 metres (65 feet)

Do not park closer to a junction than the legally required minimum distance unless you are occupying an authorised parking space. Parking any closer obscures the line of vision of other road users and makes it difficult for large trucks to turn into and out of the junction.

Q 384 You are leaving your vehicle parked on a road. When may you leave the engine running?

Mark one answer

- **A.** If you will be parked for less than five minutes
- **B.** If the battery is flat
- **C.** If there is a passenger in the vehicle
- **D.** Not on any occasion

When you stop to park, always apply the handbrake, switch off the engine and switch off the headlights. On hills you should leave your vehicle in an appropriate gear. At night you may have to leave on your sidelights or parking lights. If your car is stolen when you leave it with the engine running, your insurance company may legally refuse to settle your claim against theft or related damages.

Q 385 Your vehicle is parked on the road at night. When must you use sidelights?

Mark one answer

- **A.** Where there are continuous white lines in the middle of the road
- **B.** Where the speed limit exceeds 30mph
- **C.** Where you are facing oncoming traffic
- **D.** Where you are near a bus stop

When you park at night the headlights of oncoming traffic should cause your rear reflectors to give the drivers a red warning signal. Do not park alongside continuous whites lines or near a bus stop.

Q 386 You park overnight on a road with a 40mph speed limit. You should

Mark one answer

- **A.** Park facing the traffic
- **B.** Park with sidelights on
- **C.** Park with dipped headlights on
- **D.** Park near a street light

At night you should always park facing in the same direction as the flow of traffic. Never leave dipped headlights on – it is an offence to dazzle other road users. A caravan or trailer must be parked with lights on even if the speed limit on the road is 30mph.

Q 387 You can park on the right-hand side of a road at night

Mark one answer

- **A.** In a one-way street
- **B.** With your sidelights on
- **C.** More than 10 metres (33 feet) from a junction
- **D.** Under a lamp-post

When you drive towards a vehicle properly parked at night your headlights turn its rear reflectors into red warning lights. If the vehicle is parked partly on the pavement the reflectors could make you misjudge your road position. If the vehicle is facing you and its headlights are dirty, it presents a danger you may not see until it is too late.

Q 388 You are parked in a busy high street. What is the safest way to turn your vehicle around to go the opposite way?

Mark one answer

- **A.** Find a quiet side road to turn round in
- **B.** Drive into a side road and reverse into the main road
- **C.** Get someone to stop the traffic
- **D.** Do a U-turn

In a busy street a U-turn would be highly dangerous, if only because it involves cutting across at least two streams of traffic with one flowing in the opposite direction to the other. Reversing from a side road into a main road is not permitted because it is extremely dangerous. Don't expect a uniformed police officer or traffic warden to hold up traffic just for your sake. In a quiet side road or at the end of a cul-de-sac you can often find a safe and convenient turning circle.

Q 389 When may you reverse from a side road into a main road?

Mark one answer

- **A.** Only if both roads are clear of traffic
- **B.** Not at any time
- **C.** At any time
- **D.** Only if the main road is clear of traffic

Parked vehicles may add to your difficulties by obscuring your view of the main road and traffic requiring priority. It is foolish and illegal to reverse out of a side road into a main road.

Q 390 You must not reverse

Mark one answer

- **A.** For longer than necessary
- **B.** For more than a car's length
- **C.** Into a side road
- **D.** In a built-up area

You may reverse for more than a car's length in a built-up area and even in a one-way street if it is part of your manoeuvre to park your vehicle parallel to the kerb. You may also reverse into a side road to the left or right and continue reversing until you are at least 10m (33ft) back from the junction.

Q 391 You are on a busy main road and find that you are travelling in the wrong direction. What should you do?

Mark one answer

- **A.** Turn into a side road on the right and reverse into the main road
- **B.** Make a U-turn in the main road
- **C.** Make a 'three-point' turn in the main road
- **D.** Turn round in a side road

Never do anything that could increase the risks of an accident or force other road users to alter their speed and/or direction. A driving examiner would regard such an action as a fault. It could cause you to fail your test.

Q 392 You are approaching a busy junction. There are several lanes with road markings. At the last moment you realise that you are in the wrong lane. You should

Mark one answer

- **A.** Continue in that lane
- **B.** Force your way across
- **C.** Stop until the area has cleared
- **D.** Use clear arm signals to cut across

All actions should be preceded by the MSM routine and never left until the last moment. Never cause any inconvenience to other drivers alongside or behind.

Q 393 You are driving along a street with parked vehicles on the left-hand side. For which THREE reasons must you keep your speed down?

Mark three answers

- **A.** So that oncoming traffic can see you more clearly
- **B.** You may set off car alarms
- **C.** Vehicles may be pulling out
- **D.** Drivers' doors may open
- **E.** Children may run out from between the vehicles

Always be alert for **moving hazards**: car doors opening suddenly, vehicles moving off without indicating, young children running into the road, elderly people stepping off the pavement, etc. See **Q26** and **Q27**.

Q 394 You meet an obstruction on your side of the road. You must

Mark one answer

- **A.** Drive on: it is your right of way
- **B.** Give way to oncoming traffic
- **C.** Wave oncoming vehicles through
- **D.** Accelerate to get past first

Unless a road sign indicates otherwise, you should give priority to oncoming traffic on the opposite side of the road. Try always to select and follow a smooth safety line that will take you past any obstruction on your side of the road. Hold back but stay on your safety line if you have to give priority to oncoming vehicles. Make eye contact with the drivers but do not flash your lights or wave them on. It is up to them to decide that you have held back and that it is safe for them to proceed.

Q 395 As a car driver which THREE lanes must you NOT use?

Mark three answers

- **A.** Crawler lane
- **B.** Bus lane at the times shown
- **C.** Overtaking lane
- **D.** Acceleration lane
- **E.** Cycle lane
- **F.** Tram lane

Take care not to obstruct buses and trams, whose drivers have a timetable to follow. And take care not to endanger cyclists by driving close to or into their lane.

Q 396 You may drive a motor car in this bus lane

Mark one answer

- **A.** Outside its operation hours
- **B.** To get to the front of a traffic queue
- **C.** At no times at all
- **D.** To overtake slow-moving traffic

This traffic sign shows the times when the lane should be used by cyclists and local buses. These are also the times when the lane should not be used by other vehicles. Take care not to cross the lane line or to drive too closely past cyclists using the lane. See **Q521** and **Q522**.

Q 397 You are driving on a road that has a cycle lane. The lane is marked by a solid white line. This means that

Mark two answers

- **A.** You must not drive in the lane unless it is unavoidable
- **B.** The lane cannot be used for parking your vehicle
- **C.** You can drive in the lane at any time
- **D.** The lane must be used by motorcyclists in heavy traffic

A cycle lane should be kept free of obstructions at all times. Moped riders and motorcyclists are not allowed to ride their machines in a cycle lane even in the rush hour.

Q 398 Where may you overtake on a one-way street?

Mark one answer

- [ ] **A.** Only on the left-hand side
- [ ] **B.** Overtaking is not allowed
- [ ] **C.** Only on the right-hand side
- [ ] **D.** Either on the right or the left

If you plan to turn at the end of a one-way street, you are permitted to overtake on the left to turn left and to overtake on the right when planning to turn right. Signal and move into the appropriate lane in good time. Watch out for traffic changing lanes without warning at the last moment. See **Q102, Q180** and **Q459**.

Q 399 When going straight ahead at a roundabout you should

Mark one answer

- [ ] **A.** Indicate left before leaving the roundabout
- [ ] **B.** Not indicate at any time
- [ ] **C.** Indicate right when approaching the roundabout
- [ ] **D.** Indicate left when approaching the roundabout

Roundabouts are circular one-way streets. You join on the left, usually at give-way lines, not stop lines. You have a clear all-round view of oncoming traffic. You give priority to traffic already on the roundabout to your right. You merge without causing other vehicles to change speed and/or direction. You leave by an exit on your left. See **Q542** and **Q604**.

Q 400 At a mini-roundabout you should

Mark one answer

- [ ] **A.** Give way to traffic from the right
- [ ] **B.** Give way to traffic from the left
- [ ] **C.** Give way to traffic from the other way
- [ ] **D.** Stop even when empty

Remember that the regulations for roundabouts apply in exactly the same way at a mini-roundabout. See **Q521**.

Q 401 You are going straight ahead at a roundabout. How should you signal?

Mark one answer

- [ ] **A.** Signal right on the approach and then left to leave the roundabout
- [ ] **B.** Signal left as you leave the roundabout
- [ ] **C.** Signal left on the approach to the roundabout and keep the signal on until you leave
- [ ] **D.** Signal left just after you pass the exit before the one you'll take

As you approach a roundabout, get into the most appropriate lane for your exit. This is usually the left lane for turning left or going straight ahead or the right lane for turning right. Slow down. Unless road markings indicate otherwise, give way to traffic already on the roundabout and coming from the right.

To turn left at a roundabout:
(1) signal left on approach
(2) keep to the left on the roundabout
(3) keep signalling until you have taken your exit off the roundabout
To go straight ahead:
(1) do **not** signal on approach
(2) keep in the lane you used to join the roundabout
(3) signal left just as you pass the exit before the one you want
To turn right:
(1) signal right on approach
(2) keep to the right on the roundabout and keep signalling right
(3) signal left just as you pass the exit before the one you want

When leaving the roundabout, watch out for two-wheeled vehicles. When you have left the roundabout, cancel your signal. Apply the same rules to mini-roundabouts. See **Q399**.

Q 402 At a crossroads there are no signs or road markings. Two vehicles approach. Which has priority?

Mark one answer
- [ ] **A.** Neither vehicle
- [ ] **B.** The vehicle travelling the fastest
- [ ] **C.** The vehicle on the widest road
- [ ] **D.** Vehicles approaching from the right

Take great care at unmarked crossroads. Make eye contact with drivers of other vehicles waiting at or approaching the crossroads. Be prepared both to give them priority and to accept priority if appropriate and offered. Do not flash your lights, sound your horn or wave other road users on. See **Q582**.

Q 403 At a crossroads with no road markings who has priority?

Mark one answer
- [ ] **A.** Traffic from the left
- [ ] **B.** Traffic from the right
- [ ] **C.** Nobody
- [ ] **D.** Traffic from ahead

See **Q402** and **Q404**.

Q 404 Who has priority at an unmarked crossroads?

Mark one answer
- [ ] **A.** The driver of the larger vehicle
- [ ] **B.** No one
- [ ] **C.** The driver who is going faster
- [ ] **D.** The driver on the wider road

Who actually gives or takes priority at unmarked crossroads can depend not only upon the skill and experience of the drivers but also upon the size and manoeuvrability of their vehicles. A small car might hold back or might go forward quickly to give a large vehicle room to turn. See **Q582**.

Q 405 You are intending to turn right at a junction. An oncoming driver is also turning right. It will normally be safer to

Mark one answer

- [ ] **A.** Keep the other vehicle to your RIGHT and turn behind it (offside to offside)
- [ ] **B.** Keep the other vehicle to your LEFT and turn in front of it (nearside to nearside)
- [ ] **C.** Carry on and turn at the next junction instead
- [ ] **D.** Hold back and wait for the other driver to turn first

When traffic or a junction layout makes you pass nearside-to-nearside, watch out for oncoming vehicles hidden from view. This is a hazard especially with buses and other large vehicles.

Q 406 You may only enter a box junction when

Mark one answer

- [ ] **A.** There are less than two vehicles in front of you
- [ ] **B.** The traffic lights show green
- [ ] **C.** Your exit road is clear
- [ ] **D.** You need to turn left

Do not proceed unless your way forward is clear. This rule applies to every situation. You **must not** enter a yellow box junction until your exit is clear. But you may enter if you are only stopped from turning right by oncoming traffic or by vehicles turning right. See **Q39, Q407** and **Q408.**

Q 407 You may wait in a yellow box junction when

Mark one answer

- [ ] **A.** Oncoming traffic is preventing you from turning right
- [ ] **B.** You are in a queue of traffic turning left
- [ ] **C.** You are in a queue of traffic to go ahead
- [ ] **D.** You are on a roundabout

See **Q406.**

Q 408 You want to turn right at a box junction. You should

Mark one answer

- [ ] **A.** Wait in the box junction until your exit is clear
- [ ] **B.** Wait before the junction until it is clear of all traffic
- [ ] **C.** Drive on: you cannot turn right at box junction
- [ ] **D.** Drive slowly into the box junction when signalled by oncoming traffic

You should obey the signals of uniformed police officers and traffic wardens but not signals from other drivers, who are not authorised to control traffic. See **Q410, Q411** and **Q583–586.**

Q 409 At a pelican crossing, what does a flashing amber light mean?

Mark one answer

- **A.** You must not move off until the lights stop flashing
- **B.** You must give way to pedestrians still on the crossing
- **C.** You can move off, even if pedestrians are still on the crossing
- **D.** You must stop because the lights are about to change to red

Flashing amber lights warn of danger. You should be prepared to stop when you see them. You may also meet flashing amber lights on motorways and road maintenance vehicles as well as at railway and school crossings.

Q 410 On which THREE occasions MUST you stop your vehicle?

Mark three answers

- **A.** When involved in an accident
- **B.** At a red traffic light
- **C.** When signalled to do so by a police officer
- **D.** At a junction with double broken white lines
- **E.** At a pelican crossing when the amber light is flashing and no pedestrians are crossing

Double broken white lines across part of the road tell you to give way. An unbroken white line means stop. Double broken white lines across the whole road signify a give-way junction at the end of a one-way street. See **Q408**.

Q 411 You MUST stop when signalled to do so by which THREE of these?

Mark three answers

- **A.** A police officer
- **B.** A pedestrian
- **C.** A school crossing patrol
- **D.** A bus driver
- **E.** A red traffic light

If an unauthorised person signals you to stop, you need not stop but you should take care. There may be a good reason for the signal. You must stop at the scene of an accident in which you have been involved unless a uniformed police officer or traffic warden directs you otherwise. See **Q408**.

Q 412 When are you allowed to exceed the maximum speed limit?

Mark one answer

- **A.** Between midnight and 6am
- **B.** Never
- **C.** When overtaking
- **D.** When the road's clear

Speed limits are assigned for safety reasons. You will be committing an offence if you exceed a speed limit even if you think it is safe. See **Q413** below.

Q 413 You see this sign ahead of you. It means

Mark one answer

- [ ] **A.** Start to slow down to 30mph after passing it
- [ ] **B.** You are leaving the 30mph speed limit area
- [ ] **C.** Do not exceed 30mph after passing it
- [ ] **D.** The minimum speed limit ahead is 30mph

Remember that a **maximum** speed limit is the **highest** speed you are allowed. It is **not** a target you must achieve. Often you need to drive below the speed limit to be safe.

Q 414 If you see a 30mph limit ahead it means

Mark one answer

- [ ] **A.** That the restriction applies only during the working day
- [ ] **B.** That you must not exceed this speed
- [ ] **C.** That it is a guide and you are allowed to drive 10% faster
- [ ] **D.** That you must keep your speed up to 30mph

It is an offence to break the speed limit. If you drive 10% faster than the speed limit you will still be breaking the law. It would be no defence to blame your speedometer for being only 90% accurate.

Q 415 You are entering an area of roadworks. There is a temporary speed limit displayed. You must

Mark one answer

- [ ] **A.** Not exceed the speed limit
- [ ] **B.** Obey the limit only during rush hour
- [ ] **C.** Accept the speed limit as advisable
- [ ] **D.** Obey the limit except for overnight

When a speed limit is introduced it applies at all times of the day and night even if it is indicated by a temporary sign. A temporary speed limit for a section of roadworks should be obeyed throughout the section between the temporary sign indicating maximum speed and the sign indicating the end of the restrictions.

Q 416 While driving, you approach roadworks. You see a temporary maximum speed limit sign. You must

Mark one answer

- [ ] **A.** Comply with the sign during the working day
- [ ] **B.** Comply with the sign at all times
- [ ] **C.** Comply with the sign when the lanes are narrow
- [ ] **D.** Comply with the sign during the hours of darkness

At roadworks you should expect delays and hazards such as uneven road surfaces, ramps, contraflows, unpredictable movement of machinery and workmen, etc. See **Q415**.

Q 417 What does this sign mean?

Mark one answer
- [ ] **A.** Maximum speed limit with traffic calming
- [ ] **B.** Minimum speed limit with traffic calming
- [ ] **C.** '20 cars only' parking zone
- [ ] **D.** Only 20 cars allowed at any one time

To improve road safety and reduce the number of traffic accidents, local authorities are introducing a **maximum** speed limit of 20mph in certain residential and shopping areas as well as outside school and park entrances. These zones often have speed humps in the road. You should drive very slowly over speed humps. See **Q292** and **Q547**.

Q 418 What does this sign mean?

Mark one answer
- [ ] **A.** New speed limit 20mph
- [ ] **B.** No vehicles over 30 tonnes
- [ ] **C.** Minimum speed limit 30mph
- [ ] **D.** End of 20mph zone

Remember that a speed limit is not a target but a maximum speed to keep below. Within the limit you should match your speed to the traffic and weather conditions.

Q 419 You are driving along a road that has no traffic signs. There are street lights. What is the speed limit?

Mark one answer
- [ ] **A.** 20mph
- [ ] **B.** 30mph
- [ ] **C.** 40mph
- [ ] **D.** 60mph

A speed limit is determined by the national speed limit and by the class or type of the road and vehicle. The speed limit on a restricted road is 30mph unless otherwise indicated. A road is restricted when there are street lights not more than 200yds (185m) apart.

Q 420 Where you see street lights but no speed limit signs the limit is usually

Mark one answer
- [ ] **A.** 30mph
- [ ] **B.** 40mph
- [ ] **C.** 50mph
- [ ] **D.** 60mph

Remember that more and more 20mph zones are being established by local authorities to improve road safety in residential areas. See **Q417**.

Q 421 There are no speed limit signs on the road. How is a 30mph limit indicated?

Mark one answer

- [ ] **A.** By hazard warning lines
- [ ] **B.** By street lighting
- [ ] **C.** By pedestrian islands
- [ ] **D.** By double or single yellow lines

> You should see speed limit and repeater signs displayed if a road without street lighting is classed as restricted or one with street lighting is classed as national speed limit.

Q 422 What does a speed limit sign like this mean?

40

Mark one answer

- [ ] **A.** It is safe to drive at the speed shown
- [ ] **B.** The speed shown is the advised maximum
- [ ] **C.** The speed shown allows for various road and weather conditions
- [ ] **D.** You must not exceed the speed shown

> Remember: **circle = must** and **red = not**. A maximum speed limit sign means you must not exceed that speed.

Q 423 What is the meaning of this sign?

Mark one answer

- [ ] **A.** Local speed limit applies
- [ ] **B.** No waiting on the carriageway
- [ ] **C.** National speed limit applies
- [ ] **D.** No entry to vehicular traffic

> The Highway Code lists the maximum speed limits which apply to different types of vehicles and roads. With the possible exception of the police and certain emergency services operating under special conditions, the highest speed allowed on the public highway is 70mph. See **Q424–Q428** and **Q493, Q498** and **Q502**.

Q 424 What is the national speed limit on a single carriageway road for cars and motorcycles?

Mark one answer

- [ ] **A.** 70mph
- [ ] **B.** 60mph
- [ ] **C.** 50mph
- [ ] **D.** 30mph

> This speed limit also applies to car-derived vans. A 50mph limit applies if the car (or car-derived van) is towing a caravan or trailer.

Q 425 What is the maximum speed on a single carriageway road?

Mark one answer
- [ ] **A.** 50mph
- [ ] **B.** 60mph
- [ ] **C.** 40mph
- [ ] **D.** 70mph

The maximum speed limit is the national speed limit: see **Q423**. For cars and motorcycles on dual carriageways the maximum speed is 70mph. But if a dual carriageway becomes restricted to a single carriageway, the maximum speed limit is 60mph.

Q 426 A single carriageway road has this sign. What's the maximum permitted speed for a car towing a trailer?

Mark one answer
- [ ] **A.** 30mph
- [ ] **B.** 40mph
- [ ] **C.** 50mph
- [ ] **D.** 60mph

This speed limit also applies to car-derived vans and to goods vehicles not exceeding 7.5 tonnes maximum laden weight.

Q 427 What is the national speed limit for cars and motorcycles on a dual carriageway?

Mark one answer
- [ ] **A.** 30mph
- [ ] **B.** 50mph
- [ ] **C.** 60mph
- [ ] **D.** 70mph

Learner drivers are not allowed to drive on motorways. They are allowed to drive on dual carriageways, where they can gain valuable experience of some but not all of the problems and responsibilities of motorway-style driving.

Q 428 You are towing a small caravan on a dual carriageway. You must not exceed

Mark one answer
- [ ] **A.** 50mph
- [ ] **B.** 40mph
- [ ] **C.** 70mph
- [ ] **D.** 60mph

The higher the speed when towing a caravan, the greater is the risk of snaking. See **Q231** and **Q424**.

Q 429 You are driving in the right lane of a dual carriageway. You see signs showing that the right lane is closed 800 yards ahead. You should

In the UK the general rule of the road is: drive on the left keeping to the left. For dual carriageways and motorways the general rule is: drive in the left lane except when overtaking slower-moving traffic.

GET IN LANE

↑ ↑ ▬

800 yards

Mark one answer
- **A.** Keep in that lane until you reach the queue
- **B.** Move to the left immediately
- **C.** Wait and see which lane is moving faster
- **D.** Move to the left in good time

The higher your speed the further ahead you should look and plan your driving. Good drivers make allowances for drivers changing lanes at the last minute because of bad planning or inconsiderate driving. See **Q524, Q562** and **Q569**.

Q 430 You are driving on a two-lane dual carriageway. For which TWO of the following would you use the right-hand lane?

Mark two answers
- **A.** Turning right
- **B.** Normal driving
- **C.** Driving at the minimum allowed speed
- **D.** Constant high-speed driving
- **E.** Overtaking slower traffic
- **F.** Mending punctures

Q 431 On a three-lane dual carriageway the right-hand lane can be used for

Mark one answer
- **A.** Overtaking only, never turning right
- **B.** Overtaking or turning right
- **C.** Fast-moving traffic only
- **D.** Turning right only, never overtaking

On many dual carriageways you may turn right. This may be one of the reasons why dual carriageways are not as safe as motorways. Never call or think of the right lanes as the fast lanes. The speed limit applies equally to all lanes.

Q 432 You are going along a single-track road with passing places only on the right. The driver behind wishes to overtake. You should

Mark one answer
- **A.** Speed up to get away from the following driver
- **B.** Switch on your hazard warning lights
- **C.** Wait opposite a passing place on your right
- **D.** Drive into a passing place on your right

Q 433 You are on a road that is only wide enough for one vehicle. There is a car coming towards you. Which TWO of these would be correct?

Mark two answers

- **A.** Pull into a passing place on your right
- **B.** Force the other driver to reverse
- **C.** Pull into a passing place if your vehicle is wider
- **D.** Pull into a passing place on your left
- **E.** Wait opposite a passing place on your right
- **F.** Wait opposite a passing place on your left

> Places are usually available at intervals on single-track roads to allow vehicles to pass one another. Never treat one as lay-by. If another vehicle wishes to pass you from whichever direction, pull into a passing place on your left or stop opposite a passing place on your right. In general you should give way to uphill traffic and to vehicles much larger than your own. See **Q183** and **Q185**.

Q 434 You will see these markers when approaching

Mark one answer

- **A.** A concealed level crossing
- **B.** The end of a motorway
- **C.** A concealed 'road narrows' sign
- **D.** The end of a dual carriageway

> White countdown markers are on a blue background for motorways and on a green background for primary routes and dual carriageways. Each white bar represents 100yds (90m) to the destination (eg slip road exit). Be aware that red countdown bars may represent less than 100yds (90m), but they are spaced equally to aid judgement.

Q 435 You are driving over a level crossing. The warning lights come on and a bell rings. What should you do?

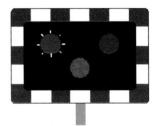

Mark one answer

- **A.** Get everyone out of the vehicle immediately
- **B.** Stop and reverse back to clear the crossing
- **C.** Keep going and clear the crossing
- **D.** Stop immediately and use your hazard warning lights

> At railway crossings, the first warning of trains coming is a bell and a steady amber light, which means stop. This warning is followed by a pair of red lights starting to flash and the barriers coming down. You should keep going if you have already crossed the white line when the amber light comes on. But you **must not** cross the line when the red lights are flashing, even if a train has gone by. It is only safe to cross when the lights go off and the barriers go up.

Q 436 You are waiting at a level crossing. The red warning lights continue to flash after a train has passed by. What should you do?

Mark one answer

- [ ] **A.** Get out and investigate
- [ ] **B.** Telephone the signal operator
- [ ] **C.** Continue to wait
- [ ] **D.** Drive across carefully

At a railway level crossing, be patient and prepared to wait for more trains. A flashing red light signals the approach of trains, which always have priority where the track crosses a road. Remain behind the white line in front of the barrier. Do not drive forward until the alarm and flashing lights are off and the barriers fully up. See **Q356–Q359**.

Q 437 You are waiting at a level crossing. A train has passed but the lights keep flashing. You must

Mark one answer

- [ ] **A.** Carry on waiting
- [ ] **B.** Phone the signal operator
- [ ] **C.** Edge over the stop line and look for trains
- [ ] **D.** Park your vehicle and investigate

See **Q436**.

Q 438 These flashing red lights mean STOP. In which THREE of the following places could you find them?

Mark three answers

- [ ] **A.** Pelican crossings
- [ ] **B.** Lifting bridges
- [ ] **C.** Zebra crossings
- [ ] **D.** Level crossings
- [ ] **E.** Motorway exits
- [ ] **F.** Fire stations

You may also see these lights at an airfield. A steady amber light and an audible alarm warn you to stop if you can do so safely. When the red lights are flashing, all traffic must stop and remain stationary until the lights go out and any barrier is raised. See **Q435–Q437**.

Q 439 Which of the following CAN travel on a motorway?

Mark one answer

- [ ] **A.** Cyclists
- [ ] **B.** Vans
- [ ] **C.** Farm tractors
- [ ] **D.** Learner drivers

Motorways provide safe routes for full licence holders driving or riding vehicles capable of travelling at speeds up to 70mph. They are not available to mopeds or to learner drivers.

Q 440 Which FOUR of these must not use motorways?

Mark four answers

- [ ] **A.** Learner car drivers
- [ ] **B.** Motorcycles over 50cc
- [ ] **C.** Double-decker buses
- [ ] **D.** Farm tractors
- [ ] **E.** Horse riders
- [ ] **F.** Cyclists

Dual carriageways may be used by agricultural vehicles, horse riders, cyclists and learner drivers. The national speed limit applies unless a lower limit is indicated. This can put road users like cyclists and horse riders at serious risk from vehicles that might pass close by at their maximum permitted speed.

Q 441 You are joining a motorway. Why is it important to make full use of the slip road?

Mark one answer

- [ ] **A.** Because there is space available to reverse if you need to
- [ ] **B.** To allow you direct access to the overtaking lanes
- [ ] **C.** To build up a speed similar to traffic on the motorway
- [ ] **D.** Because you can continue on the hard shoulder

Slip roads serve mainly as acceleration lanes and are designed to let drivers adjust their speed so they can merge into a safe gap in the traffic already on the motorway. At some junctions signs may indicate that the slip road continues as an extra lane to become part of the motorway. Give way to traffic already on the motorway. Do not leave the left lane until you have become accustomed to the speed of the motorway traffic.

Q 442 When joining a motorway you must always

Mark one answer

- [ ] **A.** Use the hard shoulder
- [ ] **B.** Stop at the end of the acceleration lane
- [ ] **C.** Come to a stop before joining the motorway
- [ ] **D.** Give way to traffic already on the motorway

Vehicles already on the motorway should assist those using the slip road by keeping their own speed steady and, if safe and convenient, should make a gap by moving out of the left lane. Traffic may sometimes be directed to drive on the hard shoulder when motorway roadworks are in progress. At all other times you must use the hard shoulder only if you have to stop in an emergency. See **Q353**.

Q 443 Immediately after joining a motorway you should normally

Mark one answer

- [ ] **A.** Try to overtake
- [ ] **B.** Readjust your mirrors
- [ ] **C.** Position your vehicle in the centre lane
- [ ] **D.** Keep in the left lane

Good drivers will smoothly adjust their speed to that of the traffic on the motorway and give themselves time to adjust to the conditions before considering the possible need to change lanes and overtake slower vehicles.

Q 444 At night, when leaving a well-lit motorway service area, you should

Mark one answer

- **A.** Drive for some time using only your sidelights
- **B.** Give your eyes time to adjust to the darkness
- **C.** Switch on your interior light until your eyes adjust
- **D.** Close your eyes for a moment before leaving the slip road

Our eyes do not adjust rapidly to changes in the light. Consequently, driving out of a dark tunnel into bright sunshine or facing the sudden glare from other vehicles' headlights at night can be particularly dangerous. A dirty windscreen can worsen the effect of the glare. See **Q548.**

Q 445 You are driving a car on a motorway. Unless signs show otherwise you must NOT exceed

Mark one answer

- **A.** 50mph
- **B.** 60mph
- **C.** 70mph
- **D.** 80mph

Do not be tempted to break the law in response to other drivers exceeding the speed limit. Keep at least a two-second gap from the vehicle in front. Remember to increase it if road and weather conditions deteriorate.

Q 446 What is the national speed limit on motorways for cars and motorcycles?

Mark one answer

- **A.** 30mph
- **B.** 50mph
- **C.** 60mph
- **D.** 70mph

The national speed limits vary with the class of road and the type of vehicle. On motorways the speed limit for a car towing a caravan or trailer is the same as that for goods vehicles exceeding 7.5 tonnes maximum laden weight.

Q 447 What is the national speed limit for cars and motorcycles in the centre lane of a three-lane motorway?

Mark one answer

- **A.** 40mph
- **B.** 50mph
- **C.** 60mph
- **D.** 70mph

The national speed limits apply equally to all lanes on a motorway unless otherwise indicated. Remember that the right-hand lane (lane 3 on a three-lane motorway) should **not** be referred to as a fast lane, even though you may use it for overtaking vehicles moving below the national speed limit in the other lanes.

Q 448 You are towing a trailer on a motorway. What is your maximum speed limit?

Mark one answer

- **A.** 40mph
- **B.** 50mph
- **C.** 60mph
- **D.** 70mph

The national speed limit for a car towing a trailer is the same for dual carriageways and motorways. For goods vehicles exceeding 7.5 tonnes maximum laden weight, the speed limit on dual carriageways is 50mph unless a lower limit is in force.

Q 449 A basic rule when driving on motorways is

Mark one answer

- **A.** Use the lane that has least traffic
- **B.** Keep to the left lane unless overtaking
- **C.** Overtake on the side that is clearest
- **D.** Try to keep above 50mph to prevent congestion

If conditions are good and you can see well ahead you should drive at a steady speed that suits you and your vehicle. Keep a safe gap from the vehicle in front. Do not exceed the speed limit. Do not obstruct faster traffic by driving slowly in the middle or outer lane. Normally you must not overtake on the left a vehicle moving slowly in the middle or outer lane.

Q 450 The left-hand lane on a three-lane motorway is for use by

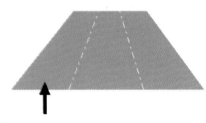

Mark one answer

- **A.** Any vehicle
- **B.** Large vehicles only
- **C.** Emergency vehicles only
- **D.** Slow vehicles only

If the left lane is occupied by slow-moving vehicles, use the lane to the right to overtake then move back into the left lane.

Q 451 The left-hand lane of a motorway should be used for

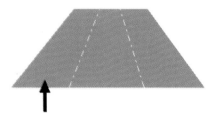

Mark one answer

- **A.** Breakdowns and emergencies only
- **B.** Overtaking slower traffic in the other lanes
- **C.** Slow vehicles only
- **D.** Normal driving

Do not confuse the left lane with the hard shoulder. Never drive on the hard shoulder unless you are directed to do so or you are pulling over to stop because of an emergency breakdown.

Q 452 You are driving on a three-lane motorway at 70mph. There is no traffic ahead. Which lane should you use?

Mark one answer

- **A.** Any lane
- **B.** Middle lane
- **C.** Right lane
- **D.** Left lane

When approaching a junction, make sure you are in the correct lane. At some junctions the left lane may take you off the motorway or on to another one.

Q 453 On a three-lane motorway which lane should you use for normal driving?

Mark one answer

- [ ] **A.** Left
- [ ] **B.** Right
- [ ] **C.** Centre
- [ ] **D.** Either the right or centre

> Use the centre lane for overtaking slower traffic in the left lane. Make sure there is enough clear space in the centre lane before you signal and change lanes to overtake.

Q 454 For what reason may you use the right-hand lane of a motorway?

Mark one answer

- [ ] **A.** For keeping out of the way of lorries
- [ ] **B.** For driving at more than 70mph
- [ ] **C.** For turning right
- [ ] **D.** For overtaking other vehicles

> On a two-lane or three-lane motorway the left lane is for normal driving and the other lanes are for overtaking slow moving traffic. Sometimes numbers are used instead of names when referring to lanes. On a three-lane motorway the left lane is lane 1, the centre lane is lane 2 and the right lane is lane 3. It is **wrong** to call lane 3 the fast lane.

Q 455 What is the right-hand lane used for on a three-lane motorway?

Mark one answer

- [ ] **A.** Emergency vehicles only
- [ ] **B.** Overtaking
- [ ] **C.** Vehicles towing trailers
- [ ] **D.** Coaches only

> The right-hand lane of a three or more lane motorway must not be used by goods vehicles with a maximum laden weight over 7.5 tonnes, or by any vehicle towing a trailer. At the time of writing all buses and coaches are prohibited from using this lane. Police and emergency vehicles may, if necessary, use the hard shoulder. See **Q454**.

Q 456 The right-hand lane of a three-lane motorway is

Mark one answer

- [ ] **A.** For lorries only
- [ ] **B.** An overtaking lane
- [ ] **C.** The right-turn lane
- [ ] **D.** An acceleration lane

> We could refer to the lanes by the numbers. The **left-hand lane** is always **lane 1** because it is the first lane we enter when joining the motorway. The **right-hand lane** is **lane 2** on a two-lane motorway, **lane 3** on a three-lane motorway, and so on. The right-hand lane is **not** the fast lane. See **Q454** and **Q455**.

Q 457 Which of the these is NOT allowed to travel in the right-hand lane of a three-lane motorway?

Mark one answer

- [ ] **A.** A small delivery van
- [ ] **B.** A motorcycle
- [ ] **C.** A vehicle towing a trailer
- [ ] **D.** A motorcycle and side-car

> You are not allowed to travel in the right-hand lane of a three-lane motorway if the national speed limit for your vehicle on motorways is 60mph. See **Q454–Q456**.

Q 458 On motorways you should never overtake on the left UNLESS

Mark one answer

- [ ] **A.** You can see well ahead that the hard shoulder is clear
- [ ] **B.** The traffic in the right-hand lane is signalling right
- [ ] **C.** You warn drivers behind by signalling left
- [ ] **D.** There is a queue of traffic to your right that is moving more slowly

When you signal left (or right) on the motorway you indicate your intention to move into the lane on your left (or right). If you are already in the left lane, your left signal indicates your intention to leave the motorway. When you have changed lanes or joined the exit slipway, you should normally cancel your signal.

Q 459 When may you NOT overtake on the left?

Mark one answer

- [ ] **A.** On a free-flowing motorway or dual carriageway
- [ ] **B.** When the traffic is moving slowly in queues.
- [ ] **C.** On a one-way street
- [ ] **D.** When the car in front is signalling to turn right

Revise these questions: **Q102, Q180, Q277, Q278, Q398** and **Q458**.

Q 460 What colour are the reflective studs between a motorway and its slip road?

Mark one answer

- [ ] **A.** Amber
- [ ] **B.** White
- [ ] **C.** Green
- [ ] **D.** Red

Think of traffic lights. The colour green indicates that you may go if your way forward is clear. On the motorway the green reflective studs tell you where you may drive.

Q 461 You are travelling on a motorway. What colour are the reflective studs on the left of the carriageway?

Mark one answer

- [ ] **A.** Green
- [ ] **B.** Red
- [ ] **C.** White
- [ ] **D.** Amber

Remember that you must not cross from the left-hand lane in order to drive along the hard shoulder. There may also be rumble studs to give you an audible warning. See **Q25**.

Q 462 On a motorway the reflective amber studs can be found between

Mark one answer

- [ ] **A.** The hard shoulder and the carriageway
- [ ] **B.** The acceleration lane and the. carriageway
- [ ] **C.** The central reservation and the carriageway
- [ ] **D.** Each pair of the lanes

You must not cross, park or stop on the central reservation. You may only stop on the hard shoulder in the event of a breakdown or real emergency.

Q 463 Where can you find reflective amber studs on a motorway?

Mark one answer

- **A.** Separating the slip road from the motorway
- **B.** On the left-hand edge of the road
- **C.** On the right-hand edge of the road
- **D.** Separating the lanes

On some motorways there may also be rumble studs to warn that you are too close to the central reservation. See **Q25**.

Q 464 Where on a motorway would you find green reflective studs?

Mark one answer

- **A.** Separating driving lanes
- **B.** Between the hard shoulder and the carriageway
- **C.** At slip road entrances and exits
- **D.** Between the carriageway and the central reservation

Green reflective studs are like green traffic lights: you may cross the line and go if your way forward is clear. White reflective studs are like your car lights: they light up the road ahead.

Q 465 You are driving on a three-lane motorway. There are red reflective studs on your left and white ones to your right. Where are you?

Mark one answer

- **A.** In the right-hand lane
- **B.** In the middle lane
- **C.** On the hard shoulder
- **D.** In the left-hand lane

White reflective studs on ordinary roads, dual carriageways and motorways serve the same purpose at night as white hazard lines do during the day. They separate streams of traffic. See **Q207**.

Q 466 What does '25' mean on this motorway sign?

Mark one answer

- **A.** The distance to the nearest town
- **B.** The route number of the road
- **C.** The number of the next junction
- **D.** The speed limit on the slip road

We should always plan our journey, especially if we know it will be a long one and we intend to travel on the motorways. Good drivers will check their atlas or road map, decide where they intend to join and leave the motorway and then note down the junction number. When they are on the motorway and preparing for their exit, they will look ahead for the junction number on the information signs. Good drivers will plan to be in the left-hand lane when they see the first sign indicating 1 mile to their exit.

Q 467 What do these motorway signs show?

Mark one answer

- **A.** They are countdown markers to a bridge
- **B.** They are distance markers to the next telephone
- **C.** They are countdown markers to the next exit
- **D.** They warn of a police control ahead

On dual carriageways, the countdown markers to an exit are white stripes on a green background. Each stripe represents 100yds (90m).

Q 468 You are intending to leave the motorway at the next exit. Before you reach the exit you should normally position your vehicle

Mark one answer

- **A.** In the middle lane
- **B.** In the left-hand lane
- **C.** On the hard shoulder
- **D.** In any lane

You should be in the correct lane ready to leave the motorway well before you see the countdown markers to your exit. If you are not in lane 1 in good time you will have to drive on to the next exit. This could cost you time and money, which a little planning and forethought could save you.

Q 469 You are driving on a motorway. By mistake, you go past the exit that you wanted to take. You should

Mark one answer

- **A.** Carefully reverse on the hard shoulder
- **B.** Carry on to the next exit
- **C.** Carefully reverse in the left-hand lane
- **D.** Make a U-turn at the next gap in the central reservation

Plan your journey on a motorway. Study a motorway map and write down the number of the exit you will take and the number of the one before it. Look for these numbers on the motorway information signs. Make sure you are in the correct lane in plenty of time to join the exit slipway you require. If you pass your exit there is no turning back.

Q 470 You are travelling in the left-hand lane of a busy motorway. Signs indicate that your lane is closed 800 yards ahead. You should

Mark one answer

- **A.** Signal right, then pull up and wait for someone to give way
- **B.** Switch on your hazard warning lights and edge over to the lane on your right
- **C.** Wait until you reach the obstruction, then move across to the right
- **D.** Move over to the lane on your right as soon as it is safe to do so

There is always more than one sign to warn of a lane closure. It is dangerous, inconsiderate driving to leave your lane change until you reach the obstruction. Be prepared to get into position early and, if necessary, to reduce speed to allow others to change lanes.

Q 471 When driving through a contraflow system on a motorway you should

Mark one answer

☐ **A.** Pull on to the hard shoulder
☐ **B.** Slow down and watch for further signals
☐ **C.** Leave at the next exit
☐ **D.** Stop and wait

Motorway signals situated on the central reservation apply to all lanes of traffic. On an overhead gantry, separate signals apply for each individual lane. Overhead flashing red lights are a serious hazard warning signal that drivers must not ignore.

Mark one answer

☐ **A.** Ensure that you do not exceed 30mph, for safety
☐ **B.** Keep a good distance from the vehicle ahead, for safety
☐ **C.** Switch lanes to keep the traffic flowing
☐ **D.** Drive close to the vehicle ahead to reduce queues

Contraflow systems and speed restrictions are introduced when essential repairs and roadworks are in progress. Cones are often used to separate lanes of traffic. Drive carefully and observe the restrictions. Watch out for workers and other pedestrians, who are always at risk in these circumstances. See **Q563**.

Q 472 You are driving on a motorway. There are red flashing lights above your lane. You must

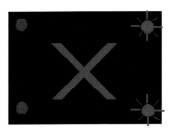

Q 473 When may you stop on a motorway?

Mark three answers

☐ **A.** If you have to read a map
☐ **B.** When you are tired and need a rest
☐ **C.** If red lights show above your lane
☐ **D.** When told to by the police
☐ **E.** If a child in the car feels ill
☐ **F.** In an emergency or a breakdown

Use the facilities at a motorway service area if you are tired and need a rest or a child in your car feels ill. If you are alone in the car and you need to check your route on a map, leave the motorway by the first available exit to find a safe and convenient place to stop. See **Q474–Q477**.

Q 474 On a motorway you may ONLY stop on the hard shoulder

Mark one answer

☐ **A.** In an emergency
☐ **B.** If you feel tired and need to rest
☐ **C.** If you accidentally go past the exit that you wanted to take
☐ **D.** To pick up a hitchhiker

If you break down, stop on the extreme left of the hard shoulder then move yourself and your passengers away on to the verge. Pedestrians are not allowed on the motorway. It is an offence to pick up or set down anyone on a slip-road or on any other part of the motorway.

Q 475 What should you use the hard shoulder of a motorway for?

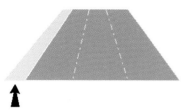

Mark one answer
- **A.** Stopping in an emergency
- **B.** Overtaking
- **C.** Stopping when you are tired
- **D.** Joining the motorway

If you stop on the motorway in an emergency, you may use the hard shoulder as an acceleration lane to rejoin the motorway when the emergency is over. See **Q476** and **Q477**.

Q 476 On the motorway the hard shoulder should be used

Mark one answer
- **A.** To answer a mobile phone
- **B.** When an emergency arises
- **C.** For a short rest when tired
- **D.** To check a road atlas

Never drive on the hard shoulder unless you are directed to do so. The hard shoulder may be the only route the police and emergency services can use to get to an accident.

Q 477 After a breakdown you need to rejoin the main carriageway of a motorway from the hard shoulder. You should

Mark one answer
- **A.** Move out on to the carriageway then build up your speed
- **B.** Move out on to the carriageway using your hazard lights
- **C.** Gain speed on the hard shoulder before moving out on to the carriageway
- **D.** Wait on the hard shoulder until someone flashes their headlights at you

Leaving the hard shoulder to rejoin the motorway is potentially a very dangerous manoeuvre. You must avoid causing traffic on the motorway to change speed and/or direction. Remember that flashing headlights only alert us to the presence of others and warn us of danger.

Q 478 You get a puncture on the motorway. You manage to get your vehicle on to the hard shoulder. You should

Mark one answer
- **A.** Change the wheel yourself immediately
- **B.** Use the emergency telephone and call for assistance
- **C.** Try to wave down another vehicle for help
- **D.** Only change the wheel if you have a passenger to help you

The police and emergency services need to keep the hard shoulder clear and they need to know that it is clear of any obstruction. If your vehicle breaks down on the motorway, your first duty is to warn other traffic and inform the motorway authorities immediately. See **Q353, Q479** and **Q480**.

Q 479 You are driving on a motorway. You have to slow down quickly due to a hazard. You should

Mark one answer
- **A.** Switch on your headlights
- **B.** Switch on your hazard lights
- **C.** Sound your horn
- **D.** Flash your headlights

Remember that you give a signal with your brake lights as soon as you press the brake pedal. Good defensive drivers are alerted by that signal.

Q 480 How should you use the emergency telephone on a motorway?

Mark one answer
- **A.** Stay close to the carriageway
- **B.** Face the oncoming traffic
- **C.** Keep your back to the traffic
- **D.** Keep your head in the kiosk

Follow the arrows on the posts at the back of the hard shoulder to get to the nearest emergency telephone. Keep as far back from the motorway as you can.

Q 481 You have broken down on a motorway. When you use the emergency telephone you will be asked

Mark three answers
- **A.** For the number on the telephone that you are using
- **B.** For your driving licence details
- **C.** For the name of your vehicle insurance company
- **D.** For details of yourself and your vehicle
- **E.** Whether you belong to a motoring organisation

The emergency telephone call you make is free. The emergency services will probably not be free. Before you drive your vehicle on motorways you should make sure that it is fit and well prepared for the journey. It is sensible and usually cheaper in the long run to be a member of a reliable motoring organisation. You can get information and advice about joining the Automobile Association at one of their information centres; you will find them at many of the major motorway service areas.

Q 482 Your vehicle has broken down on a motorway. You are not able to stop on the hard shoulder. What should you do FIRST?

Mark one answer
- **A.** Switch on your hazard warning lights
- **B.** Stop following traffic and ask for help
- **C.** Attempt to repair your vehicle quickly
- **D.** Place a warning triangle in the road

If your vehicle breaks down on the carriageway, your first priority is to warn the drivers of vehicles coming from behind you. You should stay inside your vehicle and wear your seat belt; do not leave the vehicle unless you can be certain of getting clear of the carriageway.

Q 483 You are driving on a motorway. When can you use hazard warning lights?

Mark two answers

- **A.** When a vehicle is following too closely
- **B.** When you slow down quickly because of danger ahead
- **C.** When you are towing another vehicle
- **D.** When driving on the hard shoulder
- **E.** When you have broken down, on the hard shoulder

When you switch on all four indicator lights to flash at the same time, there must be a real emergency and your vehicle must not be moving unless you are on a motorway or unrestricted dual carriageway. It is an offence to use hazard warning lights other than in an emergency. See **Q266–Q267** and **Q347–Q350**.

Q 484 Why is it particularly important to carry out a check on your vehicle before making a long motorway journey?

Mark one answer

- **A.** You will have to do more harsh braking on motorways
- **B.** Motorway service stations do not deal with breakdowns
- **C.** The road surface will wear down the tyres faster
- **D.** Continuous high speeds may increase the risk of your vehicle breaking down

Follow the manufacturer's recommendation when you adjust your tyre pressures for a heavily loaded car. Over-inflating them is illegal and results in unnecessary wear and a greater risk of accidents. Remember to make sure that the tyre on your spare wheel is correctly inflated. All your tyres must meet the minimum depth of tread requirements. It would be no defence in law to claim that they had worn down during your journey.

Q 485 You are driving on a motorway. The car ahead shows its hazard lights for a short time. This tells you that

Mark one answer

- **A.** The driver wants you to overtake
- **B.** The other car is going to change lanes
- **C.** Traffic ahead is slowing or stopping suddenly
- **D.** There is a police speed check up ahead

You may switch on all four indicator lights to flash at the same time to warn other road users of a hazard or a temporary obstruction up ahead. See **Q482**.

Q 486 You are driving on a motorway. You have to slow down quickly due to a hazard. You should

Mark one answer

- **A.** Switch on your hazard lights
- **B.** Switch on your headlights
- **C.** Sound your horn
- **D.** Flash your headlights

Good drivers aim their eyes high and look as far ahead as possible for signs of danger. On motorways, where you hope the traffic will flow unchecked, you could observe vehicles in the distance, see their brake lights come on and take this as an early hazard warning.

Q 487 What should you do when you see this sign?

Mark one answer

- [ ] **A.** Stop, ONLY if traffic is approaching
- [ ] **B.** Stop, even if the road is clear
- [ ] **C.** Stop, ONLY if children are waiting to cross
- [ ] **D.** Stop, ONLY if a red light is showing

You must stop and give way at a junction with an unbroken white line across the road. The eight-sided shape of the road sign makes it different from all other road signs and easily identified even if there is snow on it. You must stop at and behind the line. It is an offence to drive over the line without stopping. Take extra care at these dangerous junctions. See **Q508, Q509** and **Q596**.

Q 488 You MUST obey signs giving orders. These signs are mostly in

Mark one answer

- [ ] **A.** Green rectangles
- [ ] **B.** Red triangles
- [ ] **C.** Blue rectangles
- [ ] **D.** Red circles

Signs in rectangles usually give information. An important exception is the sign for one-way traffic (white arrow on a blue rectangle). Do not confuse it with the sign for ahead only (white arrow on a blue circle). Signs in triangles usually give warning. An important exception is the sign for give way (an 'upside-down' triangle – one standing on its point).

Q 489 What does this sign mean?

Mark one answer

- [ ] **A.** No parking
- [ ] **B.** No road markings
- [ ] **C.** No through road
- [ ] **D.** No entry

This sign is found at junctions with the end of one-way streets. You should watch for emerging traffic. It would be extremely dangerous and a very serious offence to cross the double broken white line and go into the one-way street against the flow of traffic.

Q 490 What does a circular traffic sign with a blue background do?

Mark one answer

- [ ] **A.** Give warning of a motorway ahead
- [ ] **B.** Give directions to a car park
- [ ] **C.** Give motorway information
- [ ] **D.** Give an instruction

A red colour warns you of danger and orders you not to do something. A blue colour is used on signs giving you an order and on motorway signs giving you information.

Q 491 What does this sign mean?

Mark one answer

- [ ] **A.** Service area 30 miles ahead
- [ ] **B.** Maximum speed 30mph
- [ ] **C.** Minimum speed 30mph
- [ ] **D.** Lay-by 30 miles ahead

A common mistake is driving too fast for the conditions. Most speed limit signs are black numbers on a white circle with a red edge. They tell you the highest speed at which you may drive. They do not tell you the safest speed to drive.

Q 492 What does this sign mean?

Mark one answer

- [ ] **A.** Minimum speed 30mph
- [ ] **B.** End of maximum speed
- [ ] **C.** End of minimum speed
- [ ] **D.** Maximum speed 30mph

On some traffic signs, a red line sloping upwards from left to right (/) cancels or crosses out what no longer applies. See **Q511** and **Q561**.

Q 493 What does this sign mean?

Mark one answer

- [ ] **A.** Waiting restrictions apply
- [ ] **B.** Waiting permitted
- [ ] **C.** National speed limit applies
- [ ] **D.** Clearway (no stopping)

Yellow lines on the kerb and at the edge of the road indicate loading and waiting restrictions. The times are usually displayed on a nearby plate or on signs at the entry to restriction zones. The general rule is the more paint, the more restrictions because of the greater danger. Double yellow lines on the road and three lines on the kerb signify no waiting, loading or unloading at any time on any day in the year. Restrictions on loading and unloading include picking up and setting down passengers. See **Q423, Q498** and **Q599**.

Q 494 What is the meaning of this sign?

Mark one answer

- [ ] **A.** No entry
- [ ] **B.** Waiting restrictions
- [ ] **C.** National speed limit
- [ ] **D.** School crossing patrol

The diagonal red line slopes downwards from left to right (\). Don't confuse this sign with others where the diagonal line slopes upwards from left to right (/). See **Q493, Q511** and **561**.

Q 495 You want to park and you see this sign. On the days and times shown you should

Mark one answer

- [ ] **A.** Park in a bay and not pay
- [ ] **B.** Park on yellow lines and pay
- [ ] **C.** Park on yellow lines and not pay
- [ ] **D.** Park in a bay and pay

Meter ZONE

Mon - Fri
8.30 am - 6.30 pm
Saturday
8.30 am - 1.30 pm

Remember that by law we have no right to park on the public highway unless a uniformed police officer or traffic warden gives us permission or we make proper use of a parking meter bay. The length and cost of authorised parking on the road will vary from place to place and with the time of year.

Q 496 What does this sign mean?

Mark one answer

- [ ] **A.** End of restricted speed area
- [ ] **B.** End of restricted parking area
- [ ] **C.** End of clearway
- [ ] **D.** End of cycle route

Zone ENDS

The diagonal lines sloping upwards from left to right are used to cancel or cross out the traffic sign which has a diagonal line sloping downwards from left to right. The clearway sign has two red diagonal lines forming a cross: see **Q497** and **Q498**. So what is used to indicate the end of a clearway?

Q 497 What does this sign mean?

Mark one answer

- [ ] **A.** Roundabout
- [ ] **B.** Crossroads
- [ ] **C.** No stopping
- [ ] **D.** No entry

See **Q498**, **Q542** and **Q560**.

Q 498 You see this sign ahead. It means

Mark one answer

- [ ] **A.** National speed limit applies
- [ ] **B.** Waiting restrictions apply
- [ ] **C.** No stopping
- [ ] **D.** No entry

The NO ENTRY sign is a horizontal white strip on a red circle. It tells you not to drive over the two broken white lines marking the exit end of a one-way street. The national speed limit sign is a diagonal black strip on a white circle. See **Q423**. The sign warning you of waiting restrictions is a diagonal red line on a blue circle with a red border. See **Q493**.

Q 499 What does this sign mean?

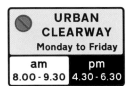

URBAN
CLEARWAY
Monday to Friday

am	pm
8.00 - 9.30	4.30 - 6.30

Mark one answer

- **A.** You can park on the days and times shown
- **B.** No parking on the days and times shown
- **C.** No parking at all from Monday to Friday
- **D.** You can park at any time: the urban clearway ends

Always check the small print on the restriction plates and parking notices when yellow line parking restrictions are in force. Ask yourself why parking is restricted and whether or not you really need to park in the restricted area.

Q 500 Which sign means 'no entry'?

Mark one answer

A. **B.** **C.** **D.**

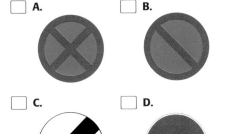

You would fail the driving test if you ignored this sign and attempted to enter a one-way street against the flow of traffic. The examiner would record a dangerous fault on his mark sheet. See **Q489**.

Q 501 Which sign means 'no stopping'?

Mark one answer

A. 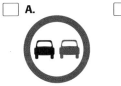 **B.**

C. 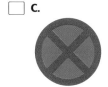 **D.**

If you have to stop in an emergency, take care that you do not cause an obstruction. See **Q497** and **Q498**.

Q 502 Which of these signs means that the national speed limit applies?

Mark one answer

A. **B.**

C. **D.**

See **Q422**. Think of the black diagonal line as cancelling or crossing out the speed limit of the restricted area you are just leaving. Remember that the maximum speed at which you may drive will depend upon the vehicle you are driving and what it may be towing. See **Q423–Q427** inclusive.

Q 503 What does this sign mean?

Mark one answer
- [ ] **A.** Distance to parking place ahead
- [ ] **B.** Distance to public telephone ahead
- [ ] **C.** Distance to public house ahead
- [ ] **D.** Distance to passing place ahead

Look for this sign if you or your passengers need a break and you are driving on a clearway. See **Q501**.

Q 504 What does this sign mean?

Mark one answer
- [ ] **A.** Vehicles may not park on the verge or footway
- [ ] **B.** Vehicles may park on the left-hand side of the road only
- [ ] **C.** Vehicles may park fully on the verge or footway
- [ ] **D.** Vehicles may park on the right-hand side of the road only

When parking consider the safety of pedestrians and other road users. Never leave the engine running or the headlights on. Park in reverse gear facing downhill and in a forward gear facing uphill.

Q 505 What does a sign with a brown background show?

Mark one answer
- [ ] **A.** Tourist directions
- [ ] **B.** Primary roads
- [ ] **C.** Motorway routes
- [ ] **D.** Minor routes

Signs for primary roads usually have a green background. Minor road signs may be black on a white background. Sometimes they have a blue border. Sometimes they are white on a blue background. See **Q529** and **Q548**.

Q 506 Traffic signs giving orders are generally which shape?

Mark one answer

- [ ] A.
- [ ] B.
- [ ] C.
- [ ] D.

Scan the road as far ahead as possible for road signs. From the shape you will know in advance if the sign will give you an order, a warning or information. This helps you to prepare in good time for any actions required on your part.

Q 507 Diamond-shaped signs give instructions to

Mark one answer
- **A.** Tram drivers
- **B.** Bus drivers
- **C.** Lorry drivers
- **D.** Taxi drivers

Don't confuse these signs with the diamond which is one of the symbols marking an emergency diversion route for motorway traffic. Look up the symbols in your Highway Code.

Q 508 What shape is a stop sign at a junction?

Mark one answer

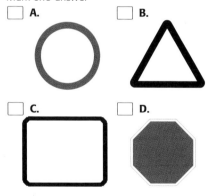

- **A.**
- **B.**
- **C.**
- **D.**

A STOP sign tells you that the junction is particularly dangerous and that you may have a very restricted view of oncoming traffic on the major road. Remember that you **must** stop **and** give way. See **Q487** and **Q596**.

Q 509 Which shape of traffic sign means that you must stop?

Mark one answer

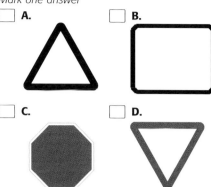

- **A.**
- **B.**
- **C.**
- **D.**

The upside-down triangle is a sign warning that you are approaching a junction where you must give way. Sometimes you will see under the sign a plate indicating the type of junction and the distance to it. See **Q487, Q533** and **Q596**.

Q 510 Which type of sign tells you NOT to do something?

Mark one answer

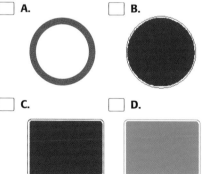

- **A.**
- **B.**
- **C.**
- **D.**

Scan the road as far ahead as possible for the colour of any road signs. This will enable you to prepare in good time for any negative or positive actions required on your part.

Q 511 What does this sign mean?

Mark one answer
- [ ] **A.** Bend to the right
- [ ] **B.** Road on the right closed
- [ ] **C.** No traffic from the right
- [ ] **D.** No right turn

At a very busy T-junction, traffic from the minor road often must turn left to avoid congestion. This sign often gives you early warning of a junction with the end of a one-way road and the prospect of traffic emerging from the right. What does this sign look like when it warns of a one-way road on the left?

Q 513 What does this sign mean?

Mark one answer
- [ ] **A.** You have priority
- [ ] **B.** No motor vehicles
- [ ] **C.** Two-way traffic
- [ ] **D.** No overtaking

Remember that there is a big difference between being entitled to priority and being given it. You cannot take your priority unless the other road users give it to you. See **Q512** and **Q516**.

Q 512 What does this sign mean?

Mark one answer
- [ ] **A.** Keep in one lane
- [ ] **B.** Priority to traffic coming towards you
- [ ] **C.** Do not overtake
- [ ] **D.** Form two lanes

Remember a **circle** means **must** and **red** means **not**. Avoid confusing this sign with the sign on a **rectangle** giving you **information** about your priority and oncoming vehicles. See **Q517** and **Q518**.

Q 514 What does this sign mean?

Mark one answer
- [ ] **A.** Do not overtake
- [ ] **B.** Oncoming cars have priority
- [ ] **C.** Two-way traffic
- [ ] **D.** No right turn ahead

Oncoming vehicles can only have priority if you give it to them. The sign ordering you to give priority to oncoming vehicles is on a white circle with a red border. See **Q512** and **Q516**. The red arrow means you **must not** take priority.

Q 515 Which sign means no overtaking?

Mark one answer

A.

B.

C.

D.

Even when overtaking is allowed, always ask yourself if you really need to overtake. If you are going to overtake, make sure it is safe and do follow the **PSL-MSM** routine. See **Q281–Q283**.

Q 517 What does this sign mean?

Mark one answer
- **A.** No overtaking
- **B.** You are entering a one-way street
- **C.** Two-way traffic ahead
- **D.** You have priority over vehicles from the opposite direction

Remember that **rectangle** usually means **information**. You have priority only when another driver gives it to you. Take care in case the drivers of oncoming vehicles ignore the sign ordering them to give you priority.

Q 516 What does this traffic sign mean?

Mark one answer
- **A.** No overtaking allowed
- **B.** Give priority to oncoming traffic
- **C.** No U-turns allowed
- **D.** One-way traffic only

Remember a **circle** means **must** and **red** means **not**. The **red** arrow in this sign means you **must not** take priority over oncoming vehicles.

Q 518 What is the meaning of this traffic sign?

Mark one answer
- **A.** End of two-way road
- **B.** Give priority to vehicles coming towards you
- **C.** You have priority over vehicles coming towards you
- **D.** Bus lane ahead

Remember **red** means **not**. The **red** arrow means oncoming traffic should **not** take priority over you.

Q 519 Which sign means 'traffic has priority over oncoming vehicles'?

Mark one answer

☐ **A.**

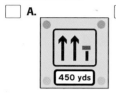

450 yds

☐ **B.**

☐ **C.**

☐ **D.**

See **Q518**.

Q 520 Which of these signs means that you are entering a one-way street?

Mark one answer

☐ **A.**

☐ **B.**

☐ **C.**

☐ **D.**

A white arrow on a blue background points in the direction you must go. An arrow pointing upwards on a **circular** sign means **ahead only** – do not turn off left or right. An arrow pointing upwards on a **rectangular** sign in a **one-way street** means go straight **ahead** (you may be allowed to turn off left or right).

Q 521 What does this sign mean?

Mark one answer

☐ **A** With-flow bus and cycle lane
☐ **B.** Contraflow bus and cycle lane
☐ **C.** No buses and cycles allowed
☐ **D.** No waiting for buses and cycles

Remember that signs on a blue background usually give positive orders. When the instructions are positive for specific vehicles and road users, they are also negative for all other vehicles and road users. If you drive in a bus and cycle lane make sure you take care and use it only at the times allowed. See **Q396, Q523** and **Q530**.

Q 522 What does this sign mean?

Mark one answer

☐ **A.** Bus station on the right
☐ **B.** Contraflow bus lane
☐ **C.** With-flow bus lane
☐ **D.** Give way to buses

You must take extra care when driving in a street with lanes which allow buses to travel against the flow of traffic. Watch for passengers getting off the bus, looking in the wrong direction for any traffic and then stepping into the road thinking it is safe. See **Q396**.

Q 523 Where would you see a contraflow bus and cycle lane?

Mark one answer
- **A.** On a dual carriageway
- **B.** On a roundabout
- **C.** On an urban motorway
- **D.** On a one-way street

> You must take extra care when you see buses and cyclists travelling in the opposite direction to all other traffic. Obey the rules for driving and overtaking in a one-way street and keep clear of any contraflow lanes. See **Q521**.

Q 524 What does this sign mean?

Mark one answer
- **A.** Turn left for parking area
- **B.** No through road on the left
- **C.** No entry for traffic turning left
- **D.** Turn left for ferry terminal

> Compare this sign with a sign warning you of a lane closure on the road ahead: see **Q429**.

Q 525 Which sign means 'no through road'?

Mark one answer

- **A.**
- **B.**
- **C.**
- **D.**

> Your practical driving test examiner will instruct you to follow the road ahead at all times unless road and traffic signs indicate otherwise or unless the examiner tells you otherwise. You could fail your test if you miss this road sign and drive into a cul-de-sac (no through road) without the examiner's instruction.

Q 526 Which sign means NO motor vehicles allowed?

Mark one answer

- **A.**
- **B.**
- **C.**
- **D.**

> A sign with a car on its own means that solo motorcycles, scooters and mopeds are allowed entry but a motorcycle with a side-car is not. When the sign is just an empty white circle with a red border, even cycles are not permitted. See **Q527**.

Q 527 Which sign means no motor vehicles are allowed?

Mark one answer

A.

B.

C.

D.

Always look at any plate beneath a sign restricting entry to a road. Sometimes certain vehicles may be allowed entry to the road for access only. In the eyes of the law, pushing a cycle is not different from riding it. Strictly speaking, you should never push a cycle over a pedestrian crossing. You should carry it. The law then regards it as a parcel.

Q 528 What does this sign mean?

Mark one answer

A. No overtaking
B. No motor vehicles
C. Clearway (no stopping)
D. Cars and motorcycles only

Cars and motorcycles are not the only motor vehicles. Buses, coaches, mopeds, tractors and other vehicles are included.

Q 529 Which type of vehicle does this sign apply to?

Mark one answer

A. Wide vehicles
B. Long vehicles
C High vehicles
D. Heavy vehicles

This sign prohibits vehicles over 4.4m (14ft 6in) in height. When the black triangles are on either side (not above and below) of, say, 2.3m (7ft 6in), the sign prohibits vehicles over that width. If the sign is a triangle (not a circle), it warns you of the maximum headroom (or width) available under a bridge (or on the road) ahead. See **Q505** and **Q548**.

Q 530 What does this sign mean?

Mark one answer

A. Give way to oncoming vehicles
B. Approaching traffic passes you on both sides
C. Turn off at the next available junction
D. Pass either side to get to the same destination

White arrows on a blue background usually show you which way to go. See **Q400 and Q521** and **Q523**.

Q 531 What does this sign mean?

Mark one answer
- **A.** Route for trams only
- **B.** Route for buses only
- **C.** Parking for buses only
- **D.** Parking for trams only

Only

You **must not** enter a lane or road reserved for trams. Remember that trams can be up to 60m (196ft) long. Always give way to trams. Never drive between a tram and the left-hand kerb at stops without platforms. Take extra care where the track crosses from one side of the road to the other, where the road narrows and where the tracks come close to the kerb. Do not park where your vehicle would obstruct trams or cause other vehicles to get in their way.

Q 532 What does this sign mean?

Mark one answer
- **A.** Route for trams
- **B.** Give way to trams
- **C.** Route for buses
- **D.** Give way to buses

Only

Trams can travel quickly and quietly but take time to start and stop. Remember that they cannot change direction to avoid traffic in their path. See **Q531** and **Q533**.

Q 533 What does this sign mean?

Mark one answer
- **A.** Wait at the barriers
- **B.** Wait at the crossroads
- **C.** Give way to trams
- **D.** Give way to farm vehicles

GIVE WAY

You will often see up ahead a white upside-down triangle painted on a minor road as you approach junctions where you must give way to traffic on the major road. See **Q509** and **Q579**.

Q 534 What are triangular signs for?

Mark one answer
- **A.** To give warnings
- **B.** To give information
- **C.** To give orders
- **D.** To give directions

Apart from the upside-down GIVE WAY triangle, you do not have to obey signs in triangles. But if you ignore any of these warning signs you do so at your peril. Many, if not most, give you advance warning of hazards ahead that are temporarily hidden from your view.

Q 535 What does this traffic sign mean?

Mark one answer
- [ ] **A.** Slippery road ahead
- [ ] **B.** Tyres liable to punctures ahead
- [ ] **C.** Danger ahead
- [ ] **D.** Service area ahead

> Triangular signs warn you of specific hazards. The sign warning you of danger ahead may have a plate underneath to indicate the nature of the danger: e.g. FALLEN TREE, HIDDEN DIP, etc. Be sure to read any plate fixed underneath a road sign.

Q 536 You are about to overtake when you see this sign. You should

Hidden dip

Mark one answer
- [ ] **A.** Overtake the other driver as quickly as possible
- [ ] **B.** Move to the right to get a better view
- [ ] **C.** Switch your headlights on before overtaking
- [ ] **D.** Hold back until you can see clearly ahead

> You may spot a dip in the road by watching traffic up ahead. Good defensive drivers will allow time for vehicles to reappear from any dip they may be hidden in. See **Q20**.

Q 537 What does this sign mean?

Mark one answer
- [ ] **A.** Two-way traffic ahead across a one-way street
- [ ] **B.** Traffic approaching you has priority
- [ ] **C.** Two-way traffic straight ahead
- [ ] **D.** Motorway contraflow system ahead

> Signs warning of changing traffic flow are very important. A pair of oppositely-facing arrows means vehicles travelling in opposite directions. If the pair of arrows is horizontal, the sign means two-way traffic ahead and across a one-way street.

Q 538 What does this sign mean?

Mark one answer
- [ ] **A.** Two-way traffic ahead
- [ ] **B.** Two-way traffic crossing a one-way street
- [ ] **C.** Two-way traffic over a bridge
- [ ] **D.** Two-way traffic crosses a two-way road

> Be careful when you drive in a one-way street that crosses a road for two-way traffic. Traffic from the two-way street may not always give you priority even if you are entitled to it.

Q 539 Which sign means 'two-way traffic crosses a one-way road'?

Mark one answer

A.

B.

C.

D.

See **Q538**.

Q 541 What does this sign mean?

Mark one answer
- **A.** Crossroads
- **B.** Level crossing with gate
- **C.** Level crossing without gate
- **D.** Ahead only

The broader line in this sign indicates that traffic on the side road should give priority to traffic on the road ahead. Good defensive drivers reduce their speed when approaching crossroads in case traffic emerges from a side road and does not give them priority.

Q 540 What does this sign mean?

Mark one answer
- **A.** Turn left ahead
- **B.** T-junction
- **C.** No through road
- **D.** Give way

On triangular warning signs for junctions, the broader black line indicates the priority through the junction. In the above sign, priority is to the left. What would the sign look like for priority to the right?

Q 542 What does this sign mean?

Mark one answer
- **A.** Ring road
- **B.** Mini-roundabout
- **C.** Restriction ends
- **D.** Roundabout

Be prepared to give way to traffic already on a roundabout. Make sure you know which exit you require so that you give the correct signals at the appropriate times. See **Q399–Q401**, **Q560** and **Q604**.

Q 543 Which of these signs means there is a double bend ahead?

Mark one answer

A.

B.

C.

D.

Good drivers use warning signs to plan their approach to a bend. The sign tells you whether you are approaching a single bend or a series of bends. It also tells you whether the bend is a left-hand or a right-hand bend. Black and white chevrons are also used if the bends are particularly sharp or dangerous.

Q 544 What does this sign mean?

Mark one answer

A. Humpback bridge
B. Traffic calming hump
C. Low bridge
D. Uneven road

When you see this sign you should take extra care, especially if you are driving a long vehicle or towing a caravan. See **Q40**.

Q 545 What does this sign mean?

Mark one answer

A. End of dual carriageway
B. Tall bridge
C. Road narrows
D. End of narrow bridge

Remember that the maximum speed allowed on a single carriageway is 10mph less than that allowed on an unrestricted dual carriageway. See **Q424–Q428**.

Q 546 Which of these signs means the end of a dual carriageway?

Mark one answer

A.

B.

C.

D.

See **Q545** above. You may see a plate under signs A and B (road narrows) when there is single-file traffic or to indicate a single-track road.

Q 547 What does this sign mean?

Mark one answer

- [ ] **A.** Humpback bridge
- [ ] **B.** Humps in the road
- [ ] **C.** Entrance to tunnel
- [ ] **D.** Steep hill upwards

> You may see this sign in residential areas where local authorities have created lower speed limit zones with traffic calming. See **Q417**.

Q 548 What does this sign mean?

Mark one answer

- [ ] **A.** Low bridge ahead
- [ ] **B.** Tunnel ahead
- [ ] **C.** Ancient monument ahead
- [ ] **D.** Accident black spot ahead

> Triangular warning signs for a low bridge usually indicate the maximum headroom. White signs on a brown background give directions to various tourist attractions. The signs often include a symbol: e.g. an elephant for a zoo. The repeat sign at a junction may just show the symbol on its own. See **Q444, Q505** and **Q529**.

Q 549 What does this sign mean?

Mark one answer

- [ ] **A.** Quayside or river bank
- [ ] **B.** Steep hill downwards
- [ ] **C.** Slippery road
- [ ] **D.** Road liable to flooding

> Triangular warning signs for steep hills may show the gradient as a percentage or as a ratio: e.g. 20% or 1:5 (one in five). The gradient is the vertical to horizontal distance. A triangular sign showing a skidding car warns you of a slippery road. You may see 'liable to flooding' below the sign: see **Q535** and **Q536**.

Q 550 What does this sign mean?

Mark one answer

- [ ] **A.** School crossing patrol
- [ ] **B.** No pedestrians allowed
- [ ] **C.** Pedestrian zone – no vehicles
- [ ] **D.** Pedestrian crossing ahead

> Remember a **circle** means **must** and **red** means **not**. A picture of a pedestrian on a white circle with a red border means no pedestrians are allowed. A picture of children on a white triangle with a red border may have a SCHOOL plate underneath. A PATROL plate tells you to be prepared to stop when you see the STOP – CHILDREN sign being held up. See **Q74–Q78**.

Q 551 > What does this sign mean?

Mark one answer
- **A.** No footpath ahead
- **B.** Pedestrians only ahead
- **C.** Pedestrian crossing ahead
- **D.** School crossing ahead

Approach any crossing with care. Be prepared to reduce speed. Remember that a pedestrian becomes entitled to absolute priority just by placing one foot on a zebra crossing. Make eye contact with the pedestrians, give a them a proper arm signal to show you are stopping, but never wave them on to the crossing. See **Q29**.

Q 552 > What does this sign mean?

Mark one answer
- **A.** Cyclists must dismount
- **B.** Bicycles are not allowed
- **C.** You are approaching a cycle route
- **D.** Walking is not allowed

Remember that signs giving **orders** are usually **circles**. Signs giving **information** are usually **rectangles**. A sign ordering pedestrians and pedal cyclists to use a segregated route is white on a circular blue background: see **Q97**.

Q 553 > What does this sign tell you?

Mark one answer
- **A.** No cycling
- **B.** Cycle route ahead
- **C.** Route for cycles only
- **D.** End of cycle route

For a 'no cycling' sign, the shape would be a circle not a triangle. A white pedal cycle on a circular blue background orders cyclists to ride on the separate route provided for their use only.

Q 554 > What does this sign mean?

Mark one answer
- **A.** Crosswinds
- **B.** Road noise
- **C.** Airport
- **D.** Adverse camber

You often see signs with a picture of a flying aircraft in the vicinity of signs with a picture of a windsock. Airports are in large, flat open areas where strong gusting winds may cause problems for aircraft on the runways and for two-wheeled or high-sided traffic on nearby roads.

Q 555 What does this sign mean?

Mark one answer
- **A.** Uneven road surface
- **B.** Bridge over the road
- **C.** Road ahead ends
- **D.** Water across the road

Before driving across a ford, check that the depth of water is not higher than the centre of your vehicle's wheels. Cross at the shallowest point. Go slowly in first gear (or low lock on an automatic car). As you cross don't change gear in case this sucks water into the exhaust. When you have crossed, make sure you dry out and test your brakes. See **Q194** and **Q322**.

Q 556 Which FOUR of these would be indicated by a triangular road sign?

Mark four answers
- **A.** Road narrows
- **B.** Ahead only
- **C.** Low bridge
- **D.** Minimum speed
- **E.** Children crossing
- **F.** T-junction

This sign may also have a plate with a message: e.g. LIABLE TO FLOODING. See **Q555**. Remember that signs on blue circles give positive instructions you must obey: see **Q491**. Do not ignore triangular signs giving warnings.

Q 557 What does this sign mean?

Mark one answer
- **A.** Railway station
- **B.** Route for cyclists
- **C.** Ring road
- **D.** Scenic route

A white picture of a cycle on a blue background indicates a cycle route. The sign may be on a circle or a rectangle. Direction signs for a railway station have a distinctive white symbol on a solid red rectangle.

Q 558 What does this sign mean?

Mark one answer
- **A.** Route for lorries
- **B.** Ring road
- **C.** Rest area
- **D.** Roundabout

A white **H** on a solid blue or red rectangle is the sign for a hospital. Blue means there are no accident services available. Red means that accident and emergency services are available but restricted times may be indicated in white. A black **HR** on a solid yellow rectangle is the sign for a holiday route: see **Q559**.

Q 559 What does this sign mean?

Mark one answer
- **A.** Hilly road
- **B.** Humps in road
- **C.** Holiday route
- **D.** Hospital route

See **Q547** for humps in the road. A white **H** on a solid blue or red rectangle means hospital ahead: see **Q558**.

Q 561 What does this sign mean?

Mark one answer
- **A.** No motor vehicles
- **B.** End of motorway
- **C.** No through road
- **D.** End of bus lane

A red diagonal line may cancel a sign: no left turn, no right turn, no U-turn, traffic lights not working, end of minimum speed, etc. Do not confuse these signs with those for clearway and for parking restrictions. See **Q492–Q495, Q498** and **Q581**.

Q 560 Which is the sign for a ring road?

Mark one answer

A.

B.

C.

D.

See **Q497, Q498** and **Q542**.

Q 562 What does this sign mean?

Mark one answer
- **A.** The right-hand lane ahead is narrow
- **B.** Right-hand lane for buses only
- **C.** No turning to the right
- **D.** The right-hand lane is closed

The number and position of the arrows and red bars will vary according to which lanes are temporarily open or closed. A horizontal red bar at the top of a vertical white bar on a solid blue rectangle is the sign for a permanent no through road. See **Q429** and **Q569**.

Q 563 What does this sign mean?

Mark one answer
- **A.** Change to the left lane
- **B.** Leave at the next exit
- **C.** Contraflow system
- **D.** One-way street

Temporary speed limits and alternative lanes may be introduced for carriageway maintenance and repairs. Make sure you obey the speed limit. See **Q471**.

Q 564 What does this motorway sign mean?

Mark one answer
- **A.** Temporary minimum speed 50mph
- **B.** No services for 50 miles
- **C.** Obstruction 50 metres (165 feet) ahead
- **D.** Temporary maximum speed 50mph

On urban motorways, overhead gantries can carry matrix light signs for each individual lane. On rural motorways the signs are fixed in the central reservations and apply to the traffic in all lanes. These signs are normally 2 miles (3km) apart. These matrix light signs are designed to give temporary and changing signals.

Q 565 You are driving on a motorway. There is a slow-moving vehicle ahead. On the back you see this sign. You should

Mark one answer
- **A.** Pass on the right
- **B.** Pass on the left
- **C.** Leave at the next exit
- **D.** Drive no further

When you see work being done on the motorway, watch for workmen on the road, contraflows and temporary speed limit signs. Be especially careful when obeying direction signs and overtaking maintenance vehicles. See **Q35**.

Q 566 What does this motorway sign mean?

Mark one answer
- **A.** Change to the lane on your left
- **B.** Leave the motorway at the next exit
- **C.** Change to the opposite carriageway
- **D.** Pull up on the hard shoulder

The motorway matrix light sign instructing you to leave the motorway at the next exit is an arrow bent upwards and pointing to the left. You must not confuse it with the sign telling you to change lanes.

Q 567 On a motorway this sign means

Mark one answer

- [ ] **A.** Move over on to the hard shoulder
- [ ] **B.** Pass a temporary obstruction on the left
- [ ] **C.** Leave the motorway at the next exit
- [ ] **D.** Move to the lane on your left

> A sign telling you to change lanes might instruct you to move into the lane on your right or your left. Note which way the arrow is pointing. And don't forget to check your mirror and signal before you change lanes. Move as soon as possible but only when it is safe.

Q 569 What does this sign mean?

Mark one answer

- [ ] **A.** Through traffic to use left lane
- [ ] **B.** Right-hand lane T-junction only
- [ ] **C.** Right-hand lane closed ahead
- [ ] **D.** 11-tonne weight limit

> This is a typical matrix light sign used on some motorways and dual carriageways to warn drivers of danger or problems up ahead. See **Q429** and **Q562**.

Q 568 You are travelling along a motorway. You see this sign. You should

Mark one answer

- [ ] **A.** Leave the motorway at the next exit
- [ ] **B.** Turn left immediately
- [ ] **C.** Change lane
- [ ] **D.** Move on to the hard shoulder

> This matrix light sign may appear on an overhead gantry or in the central reservation. Don't confuse it with a similar overhead gantry sign ordering you to move into the lane on your left. Remember that lane 1 (the left lane) is the lane for normal driving and for approaching your exit slip road.

Q 570 You are driving on a motorway. Red flashing lights appear above your lane. What should you do?

Mark one answer

- [ ] **A.** Continue in that lane and await further information
- [ ] **B.** Go no further in that lane
- [ ] **C.** Drive on to the hard shoulder
- [ ] **D.** Stop and wait for an instruction to proceed

> You must never ignore flashing red lights. They always mean danger. Remember that at railway crossings the flashing red lights mean that you must stop because trains are approaching. Matrix light signs do not issue further instructions but they do provide warnings on weather and road conditions ahead.

Q 571 A red traffic light means

Mark one answer

- **A.** You should stop unless turning left
- **B.** Stop, if you are able to brake safely
- **C.** You must stop and wait behind the stop line
- **D.** Proceed with caution

An illuminated red traffic light has only one meaning. It is extremely dangerous and a very serious offence to ignore it. Remember that even when the traffic lights show green you must not go unless it is safe and your way forward is clear.

Q 572 A red traffic light means

Mark one answer

- **A.** You must stop behind the white stop line
- **B.** You may drive straight on if there is no other traffic
- **C.** You may turn left if it is safe to do so
- **D.** You must slow down and prepare to stop if traffic has started to cross

Make sure you know the sequence of traffic light signals. If you plan your driving carefully you can often arrive at a junction when the traffic lights are showing green. Remember that from a distance you can tell traffic lights from pelican crossing lights by the amber light. Traffic lights show steady red and amber before turning green, while the pelican crossing lights flash amber before the green light shows.

Q 573 You are approaching a red traffic light. The signal will change from red to

Mark one answer

- **A.** Red and amber, then green
- **B.** Green, then amber
- **C.** Amber, then green
- **D.** Green and amber, then green

At a pelican crossing when the red light changes to flashing amber, vehicles may proceed if the crossing is clear or any pedestrians are out of danger. There is no flashing amber light at a toucan crossing.

Q 574 You are approaching traffic lights. Red and amber are showing. This means

Mark one answer

- **A.** Pass the lights if the road is clear
- **B.** There is a fault with the lights – take care
- **C.** Wait for the green light before you pass the lights
- **D.** The lights are about to change to red

Only a green traffic light means you may go but even then you must be sure that it is safe to proceed. Remember to watch out for traffic 'jumping the lights'. Listen as well as look for the possibility of police vehicles, ambulances and other vehicles driving through the traffic lights to an emergency.

Q 575 You are at a junction controlled by traffic lights. When should you NOT proceed at green?

Mark one answer
- **A.** When pedestrians are waiting to cross
- **B.** When your exit from the junction is blocked
- **C.** When you think the lights may be about to change
- **D.** When you intend to turn right

You give priority to pedestrians when they are on a crossing or in danger on the road. Remember also the general rule that you should not proceed unless it is safe and your way forward is clear.

Q 576 At traffic lights, amber on its own means

Mark one answer
- **A.** Prepare to go
- **B.** Go if the way is clear
- **C.** Go if no pedestrians are crossing
- **D.** Stop at the stop line

At traffic lights the steady amber light on its own will always be followed by the red light. You may go through the amber light if it comes on after you have crossed the stop line. You should plan your approach and arrive at a sensible speed. But if you are so close to the line that you might cause an accident by pulling up, you may go through the amber. Bear in mind the possibility of crossing traffic moving off when red and amber are still showing together.

Q 577 You see this traffic light ahead. Which light(s) will come on next?

Mark one answer
- **A.** Red alone
- **B.** Red and amber together
- **C.** Green and amber together
- **D.** Green alone

Green and amber lights at traffic signals never show at the same time. When red and amber show together you can prepare to move off when they have changed to green and your way forward is safe and clear.

Q 578 You are in the left-hand lane at traffic lights. You are waiting to turn left. At which of these traffic lights must you NOT move on?

Mark one answer
- **A.**
- **B.**
- **C.**
- **D.**

You may see an arrow on the green light indicating the direction you must follow. You may also see extra green lights with arrows to control traffic filtering left or right at the junction. When there is more than one set of lights, make sure you understand which ones apply to you.

Q 579 You're driving along a road and you see this signal. It means

Remember that a red diagonal line may cancel a sign: end of motorway, no left turn, no right turn, no U-turn, etc. Do not confuse this with the diagonal line on the sign warning of parking restrictions in force. See **Q492–Q495, Q498** and **Q561**.

Mark one answer
- **A.** Cars must stop
- **B.** Trams must stop
- **C.** Both trams and cars must stop
- **D.** Both trams and cars can continue

Remember that a green traffic light means go only if your way forward is clear and it is safe to proceed. See **Q533** and **Q575**.

Q 580 Signals are normally given by direction indicators and

Mark one answer
- **A.** Brake lights
- **B.** Side lights
- **C.** Fog lights
- **D.** Interior lights

Remember that it is an offence to drive if your brake lights do not work: see **Q250**.

Q 581 What does this sign mean?

Mark one answer
- **A.** Traffic lights out of order
- **B.** Amber signal out of order
- **C.** Temporary traffic lights ahead
- **D.** New traffic lights ahead

Q 582 When traffic lights are out of order, who has priority?

Mark one answer
- **A.** Traffic going straight on
- **B.** Traffic turning right
- **C.** Nobody
- **D.** Traffic turning left

See **Q402–Q404**.

Q 583 You approach a junction. The traffic lights are not working. A police officer gives this signal. You should

Mark one answer
- **A.** Turn left only
- **B.** Turn right only
- **C.** Stop level with the officer's arm
- **D.** Stop at the stop line

Police officers or traffic wardens will raise and move their arm as a signal for you to move. They will hold up but not move their arm as a signal for you to stop. Their arm is vertical for traffic in front of them and horizontal for traffic behind them. See **Q408, Q410, Q411, Q584** and **Q586**.

Q 584 What does this signal, from a police officer, mean to oncoming traffic?

Mark one answer
- [ ] **A.** Go ahead
- [ ] **B.** Stop
- [ ] **C.** Turn left
- [ ] **D.** Turn right

Q 585 There is a police car following you. The police officer flashes the headlights and points to the left. What should you do?

Mark one answer
- [ ] **A.** Turn at the next left
- [ ] **B.** Pull up on the left
- [ ] **C.** Stop immediately
- [ ] **D.** Move over to the left

Uniformed police officers have the authority to stop anyone at any time. To attract a motorist's attention, the officer may flash the headlamps or the blue light and/or sound the siren. To signal to the motorist to pull over, the officer may point to the left and switch on the left indicator. It is an offence not to stop when directed. But if for some reason you feel threatened or in danger, you should aim for the nearest police station or public place before actually stopping.

Q 586 How will a police officer in a patrol vehicle get you to stop?

Mark one answer
- [ ] **A.** Flash the headlights, indicate left and point to the left
- [ ] **B.** Wait until you stop, then approach you
- [ ] **C.** Use the siren, overtake, cut in front and stop
- [ ] **D.** Pull alongside you, use the siren and wave you to stop

Police drivers normally use the siren and flashing blue lights in an emergency to warn other road users. They could be hurrying to the scene of an accident. The flashing blue light indicates that you should give the police car priority. Slow down and move over to make way for them and any emergency services following them. When escorting vehicles with wide loads, police normally use only flashing blue lights and headlamps to warn traffic.

Q 587 When motorists flash their headlights at you it means

Mark one answer
- [ ] **A.** That there is a radar speed trap ahead
- [ ] **B.** That they are giving way to you
- [ ] **C.** That they are warning you of their presence
- [ ] **D.** That there is something wrong with your vehicle

You will confuse and endanger other road users by flashing your headlights unless you are drawing their attention to your presence because there is a threat of danger. It is an offence to warn other motorists of a speed trap. See **Q132**, **Q160–Q163** and **Q172**.

Q 588 You are waiting at a T-junction. A vehicle is coming from the right with the left signal flashing. What should you do?

Mark one answer

- **A.** Move out and accelerate hard
- **B.** Wait until the vehicle starts to turn in
- **C.** Pull out before the vehicle reaches the junction
- **D.** Move out slowly

A flashing indicator may or may not be a signal of the driver's intention to change speed and or direction. Drivers can and do occasionally forget to cancel an unwanted signal.

Q 589 You want to turn right at a junction but you think that your indicators cannot be seen clearly. What should you do?

Mark one answer

- **A.** Get out and check if your indicators can be seen
- **B.** Stay in the left-hand lane
- **C.** Keep well over to the right
- **D.** Give an arm signal as well as an indicator signal

When turing at a junction, always consider the possibility of giving a proper arm signal to make your intentions clear.

Q 590 Why should you make sure that you have cancelled your indicators after turning?

Mark one answer

- **A.** To avoid flattening the battery
- **B.** To avoid misleading other road users
- **C.** To avoid dazzling other road users
- **D.** To avoid damage to the indicator relay

Remember that your signal is meant to indicate to other road users what you intend to do. Imagine you are at a junction waiting to drive from a side road on to a main road. A vehicle on the main road is approaching from the right. You would find it confusing if the vehicle's left indicator had never been cancelled, or came on just before the vehicle reached your junction.

Q 591 The driver of the car in front is giving this arm signal. What does it mean?

Mark one answer

- **A.** The driver is slowing down
- **B.** The driver intends to turn right
- **C.** The driver wishes to overtake
- **D.** The driver intends to turn left

When you give **arm** signals, do them properly. Make sure other road users can see clearly whether you are going to slow down or turn left.

Q 592 The driver of this car is giving a hand signal. What is he about to do?

Mark one answer
- **A.** Turn to the left
- **B.** Turn to the right
- **C.** Go straight ahead
- **D.** Let pedestrians cross

> Note that the Highway Code refers to this as an **arm** signal. If you intend to signal to pedestrians at a crossing that you are slowing down to stop, make sure you give a proper arm signal. Do not just wave your hand through the window. See **Q594**.

Q 593 Which arm signal tells a following vehicle that you intend to turn left?

Mark one answer

A.

B.

C.

D.

> Remember that you use only your right arm to signal to traffic behind you.

Q 594 You are approaching a zebra crossing where pedestrians are waiting. Which arm signal might you give?

Mark one answer

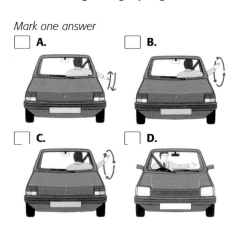

A.

B.

C.

D.

> Whether or not you give an arm signal, you should make eye contact with other road users, especially pedestrians at a crossing. Remember not to wave pedestrians across a crossing. They must check for themselves whether it is safe to step into the road. See **Q139–Q142**.

Q 595 When may you sound the horn on your vehicle?

Mark one answer
- **A.** To give you right of way
- **B.** To attract a friend's attention
- **C.** To warn other drivers of your presence
- **D.** To make slower drivers move over

> Revise these questions: **Q82–Q89, Q104, Q124, Q126, Q134, Q141, Q159, Q161, Q172, Q182, Q199, Q246, Q269** and **Q272**.

Q 596 At this junction there is a stop sign with a solid white line on the road surface. Why is there a stop sign here?

Mark one answer

- **A.** Speed on the major road is de-restricted
- **B.** It is a busy junction
- **C.** Visibility along the major road is restricted
- **D.** There are hazard warning lines in the centre of the road

When you see the eight-sided STOP sign, you **must stop** at the line when you reach the junction. After you have stopped, you may have to inch your way forward in order to check that it is safe to proceed. You must always give way to traffic on the major road. See **Q487, Q508** and **Q509**.

Q 597 You see this line across the road at the entrance to a roundabout. What does it mean?

Mark one answer

- **A.** Give way to traffic from the right
- **B.** Traffic from the left has right of way
- **C.** You have right of way
- **D.** Stop at the line

In general, roundabouts at junctions are designed to keep traffic flowing freely. On mini-roundabouts the junctions are marked with a broken white line.

Q 598 A white line like this along the centre of the road is a

Mark one answer

- **A.** Bus lane marking
- **B.** Hazard warning
- **C.** 'Give way' marking
- **D.** Lane marking

White lines along the middle of the road are meant to separate the traffic. You should not straddle or cross a single broken line, with long markings and short gaps, unless you can see that the road is clear well ahead. You must not cross a double solid white line except in specific allowable circumstances. Very often these hazard lines are reinforced by reflective studs which show up in your headlight beam at night. See **Q602**.

Q 599 What do these zigzag lines at pedestrian crossings mean?

Mark one answer

- **A.** No parking at any time
- **B.** Parking allowed only for a short time
- **C.** Slow down to 20mph
- **D.** Sounding horns is not allowed

You must not park on zigzag lines, nor stop to pick up or set down even a passenger who is disabled. Revise these questions: **Q31, Q136, Q137, Q493** and **Q380**.

Q 600 Which is a hazard warning line?

Mark one answer

☐ **A.**

☐ **B.**

☐ **C.**

☐ **D.**

Do not confuse white lane markings with hazard warning lines. Lane markings separate streams of traffic travelling in the same direction. Hazard warning lines separate streams of traffic travelling in the opposite direction.

Q 601 What does this road marking mean?

Mark one answer
☐ **A.** Do not cross the line
☐ **B.** No stopping allowed
☐ **C.** You are approaching a hazard
☐ **D.** No overtaking allowed

A broken white line across a road warns you to give way to traffic on the major road. A broken white line along the middle of a road warns you to keep clear of traffic coming towards you on the other side of the road.

Q 602 When may you cross a double solid white line in the middle of the road?

Mark one answer
☐ **A.** To pass traffic that is queuing back at a junction
☐ **B.** To pass a car signalling to turn left ahead
☐ **C.** To pass a road maintenance vehicle travelling at 10mph or less
☐ **D.** To pass a vehicle that is towing a trailer

A double solid white line along the middle of the road is the strongest warning of danger from traffic approaching from the opposite direction. You may cross it to get in and out of premises, to turn into a side road or to avoid a stationary obstruction. You may also straddle or cross a double solid white line to overtake a pedal cyclist or a horse and rider, but not a tractor travelling at less than 10mph.

Q 603 What does this sign mean?

Crawler lane

Mark one answer
☐ **A.** Leave motorway at next exit
☐ **B.** Lane for heavy and slow vehicles
☐ **C.** All lorries use the hard shoulder
☐ **D.** Rest area for lorries

Good defensive drivers keep their distance and patiently follow a large, slow-moving vehicle until they can overtake safely: see **Q34**. You often find a crawler lane on very steep hills, which large, heavily-laden lorries climb extremely slowly in their lowest gear.

Q 604 Where would you find this road marking?

Mark one answer

- **A.** At a railway crossing
- **B.** At a junction
- **C.** On a motorway
- **D.** On a pedestrian crossing

When you are approaching junctions and traffic lights, look on the road ahead for any arrows indicating the direction of traffic flow. Good drivers spot these early to avoid being trapped in the wrong lane. See **Q399–Q401** and **Q542**.

Q 605 Where would you see this road marking?

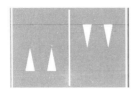

Mark one answer

- **A.** At traffic lights
- **B.** On road humps
- **C.** Near a level crossing
- **D.** At a box junction

In residential areas, zones with traffic calming improve road safety, because drivers must go very slowly to avoid damaging the wheels and suspension of their vehicles. The greater the speed at which a car hits a pedestrian, the more severe are the injuries caused and the greater is the risk of the pedestrian being killed. See **Q100**.

Q 606 Where would you see these road markings?

Mark one answer

- **A.** At a level crossing
- **B.** On a motorway slip road
- **C.** At a pedestrian crossing
- **D.** On a single-track road

For safety reasons, on some roads white hatch markings are used to widen the gap between a pair of solid white lines. You should not straddle or cross the white lines and hatch markings or chevrons except in an emergency.

Q 607 Bells hanging high across the road surface are warning you

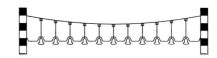

Mark one answer

- **A.** That you are approaching a high bridge
- **B.** Of overhanging trees
- **C.** Of overhead electrified cables
- **D.** That you are approaching a level crossing

These bells sound a warning when struck by a vehicle that exceeds the safe height beneath overhead electrified cables.

Alertness

1 A	2 A	3 D	4 D	5 A	6 B	7 A	8 C	9 C
10 B	11 D	12 C	13 A	14 D	15 D	16 C	17 D	18 ACE
19 B	20 D	21 A	22 A	23 C				

Hazard awareness

24 D	25 DE	26 AEF	27 BF	28 B	29 D	30 CD	31 A	32 C
33 B	34 A	35 D	36 A	37 C	38 D	39 A	40 BDF	41 C
42 A	43 C	44 A	45 B	46 C	47 D	48 ABD	49 CD	50 ABE
51 A	52 A	53 A	54 A	55 C	56 B	57 B	58 A	59 B
60 C	61 AB	62 A	63 C	64 D	65 ABC	66 ABD	67 ABC	68 C
69 C	70 D	71 C	72 C	73 B				

Vulnerable road users

74 D	75 C	76 A	77 D	78 D	79 D	80 C	81 D	82 C
83 CD	84 D	85 D	86 D	87 C	88 D	89 C	90 B	91 B
92 B	93 D	94 D	95 B	96 B	97 D	98 D	99 C	100 C
101 C	102 A	103 C	104 D	105 D	106 C	107 AC	108 C	109 D
110 C	111 B	112 B	113 B	114 D	115 B	116 B	117 A	118 C
119 A	120 C	121 B	122 A	123 C	124 D	125 A	126 ABE	127 B
128 A	129 A	130 B	131 D	132 C	133 D	134 C	135 ABC	136 AD
137 B	138 ABE	139 B						

Attitude

140 A	141 A	142 B	143 B	144 A	145 C	146 B	147 AD	148 D
149 D	150 BD	151 DF	152 D	153 B	154 A	155 BCD	156 ABE	157 B
158 D	159 A	160 D	161 C	162 D	163 D	164 A	165 C	166 C
167 B	168 D	169 D	170 C	171 A	172 B			

Vehicle Handling

173 C	174 C	175 D	176 C	177 D	178 BD	179 B	180 ACE	181 A
182 C	183 A	184 B	185 BE	186 ABD	187 D	188 A	189 AE	190 D
191 B	192 C	193 B	194 D	195 B	196 C	197 A	198 D	199 CD
200 D	201 D	202 B	203 A	204 B	205 D	206 D	207 C	208 A
209 D	210 A	211 D	212 A	213 C	214 CE	215 D	216 D	217 C
218 A	219 C							

Vehicle loading

220 AEF	221 D	222 C	223 A	224 C	225 A	226 A	227 B	228 B
229 B	230 AD	231 A	232 B	233 D	234 A			

Safety and your vehicle

235 B	236 D	237 A	238 D	239 D	240 D	241 D	242 BC	243 AB
244 A	245 CDE	246 BCDF	247 AD	248 B	249 A	250 C	251 D	252 D
253 A	254 C	255 B	256 C	257 D	258 D	259 D	260 B	261 D
262 D	263 B	264 D	265 D	266 A	267 B	268 C	269 C	270 D
271 B								

Other types of vehicle

272 BC	273 A	274 B	275 B	276 D	277 D	278 C	279 A	280 B
281 D	282 D	283 B	284 A	285 B	286 B	287 D	288 ABC	289 B
290 B								

Safety margins

291 C	292 C	293 D	294 A	295 B	296 AD	297 C	298 C	299 BC
300 D	301 B	302 B	303 B	304 A	305 C	306 C	307 D	308 B
309 D	310 D	311 C	312 B	313 C	314 D	315 A	316 C	317 C
318 D	319 B	320 B	321 D	322 D	323 C	324 D	325 D	326 D
327 B	328 C	329 A	330 D	331 D	332 C	333 BD	334 D	

Accidents

335 BE	336 B	337 C	338 B	339 ABE	340 ABE	341 BCDE	342 ABCE	343 A
344 B	345 C	346 C	347 A	348 A	349 AB	350 BCD	351 A	352 A
353 C	354 CD	355 CE	356 C	357 A	358 A	359 ABD		

Documents

360 C	361 D	362 C	363 ABD	364 C	365 C	366 CDE	367 D	368 CD
369 B	370 C	371 C	372 D	373 BE	374 B	375 ABF	376 D	

Rules of the road

377 AD	378 ABD	379 BDEF	380 C	381 D	382 A	383 A	384 D	385 B
386 B	387 A	388 A	389 B	390 A	391 D	392 A	393 CDE	394 B
395 BEF	396 A	397 AB	398 D	399 A	400 A	401 D	402 A	403 C
404 B	405 A	406 C	407 A	408 A	409 B	410 ABC	411 ACE	412 B
413 C	414 B	415 A	416 B	417 A	418 D	419 B	420 A	421 B
422 D	423 C	424 B	425 B	426 C	427 D	428 D	429 D	430 AE
431 B	432 C	433 DE	434 A	435 C	436 C	437 A	438 BDF	

Motorway rules

439 B	440 ADEF	441 C	442 D	443 D	444 B	445 C	446 D	447 D
448 C	449 B	450 A	451 D	452 D	453 A	454 D	455 B	456 B
457 C	458 D	459 A	460 C	461 B	462 C	463 C	464 C	465 D
466 C	467 C	468 B	469 B	470 D	471 B	472 D	473 CDF	474 A
475 A	476 B	477 C	478 B	479 B	480 B	481 ADE	482 A	483 BE
484 D	485 C	486 A						

Road and traffic signs

487 B	488 D	489 D	490 D	491 C	492 C	493 A	494 B	495 D
496 B	497 C	498 C	499 B	500 D	501 B	502 D	503 A	504 C
505 A	506 D	507 A	508 D	509 C	510 A	511 D	512 C	513 D
514 A	515 B	516 B	517 D	518 C	519 C	520 B	521 A	522 B
523 D	524 B	525 C	526 B	527 B	528 B	529 C	530 D	531 A
532 A	533 C	534 A	535 C	536 D	537 C	538 B	539 B	540 B
541 A	542 D	543 B	544 A	545 A	546 D	547 B	548 B	549 A
550 D	551 C	552 C	553 B	554 A	555 D	556 ACEF	557 C	558 B
559 C	560 C	561 B	562 D	563 C	564 D	565 B	566 A	567 D
568 A	569 C	570 B	571 C	572 A	573 A	574 C	575 B	576 D
577 A	578 A	579 B	580 A	581 A	582 C	583 D	584 B	585 B
586 A	587 C	588 B	589 D	590 B	591 D	592 A	593 A	594 A
595 C	596 C	597 A	598 B	599 A	600 B	601 C	602 C	603 B
604 B	605 B	606 B	607 C					

THE DRIVING TEST - **PASS FIRST TIME**